£1.00

Keith Miles was the finest swordsman in all Wales
until he was deported under armed guard for
educational reasons. He discovered at Oxford that
the pen – if not mightier than the sword – fitted
more easily into his top pocket. Since then he has
worked continuously in television, radio, theatre,
films, publishing, journalism and the Sandwich-
Welding Department of British Rail. He now
divides his time between writing, wishful thinking
and searching for a rotten borough to represent in
Parliament. *The Finest Swordsman In All France*
has been compiled from random snatches of
conversation overheard on a crowded double-
decker bus in the Cromwell Road. Keith Miles is
the author of several books and a Celtic telephone
directory. He also holds the record for not being
mentioned in any published edition of a Guinness
Book. Unknown to his wife and two children,
Keith Miles is a pseudonym.

D0774859

THE FINEST SWORDSMAN IN ALL FRANCE

A Celebration of the Cliché

KEITH MILES

I'VE HEARD OF CLICHÉS, BUT THIS IS RIDICULOUS!

SPHERE BOOKS LIMITED
London and Sydney

First published in Great Britain by
Sphere Books Ltd 1984
30-32 Gray's Inn Road, London WC1X 8JL
Copyright © by Keith Miles 1984
Cartoon copyright © by David Austen 1984

**TRADE
MARK**

Set in Baskerville

Printed and bound in Great Britain by
Collins, Glasgow

For Mark and Mindy
as a belated wedding present

Contents

Prologue

Armand: To defend your honour and to prove my undying love, I have challenged the scoundrel to a duel.

Sophie: You reckless fool, Armand! He is the finest swordsman in all France.

Armand: That one-eyed dwarf with his arm in a sling?

Sophie: He is a master of disguise. O, my brave darling! We must escape at once.

Armand: But the castle is surrounded and every exit is guarded day and night by cruel mercenaries in the pay of the Cardinal.

Sophie: There is a way out if we can but find it. These old places are honeycombed with passages. . .

Preface

Unaccustomed as I am to public speaking, it is a great privilege and pleasure for me to introduce a book, which, in actual fact, needs no introduction. At bottom, the crux of the matter, in a nutshell, is this: in all honesty, I cannot speak too highly of *The Finest Swordsman In All France*.

Far be it from me to blow my own trumpet at this juncture, but I think I may say without fear of contradiction, that, here and now, just like that, give or take a word or two, it is on the cards that the man in the street and the woman of the world will find a wealth of information about English as she is spoke if they read this slim volume, which, by common consent, is unsurpassed by any adventure story in recent years. Do not miss the boat, make a hash of it, go down the drain or play second fiddle. Buy now to avoid disappointment.

The Finest Swordsman In All France is no mere *tour de force*. Without a word of a lie, it is a classic of its kind with a rare gift for the haunting phrase. Enjoy this unique experience at face value. It is the book of the century. Its mission: to explore old words, to boldly go where every man has been before . . .

Destined to be a bestseller, here is a work that puts the tip of the iceberg into proper perspective and takes the rough with the smooth lying down. It deals with the bread and butter issues and has many irons in the fire. This is what writing is all about!

Why say *no* when you could say *maybe*?

Foreword

The origin of the cliché is lost in the mists of time. By its very nature, it is a bone of contention. How do you define it? A cliché is neither fish, flesh nor fowl and yet it is animal, vegetable and mineral. For the most part it is long and short and tall, speaks with many tongues, and is all colours of the rainbow. With eyes like a hawk, it is still as blind as a bat; though as beautiful as a buttercup, it remains as ugly as sin. It consorts with cant, slang and vulgarisms. It has a fling with proverbs, sayings and euphemisms. It courts quotations. It shares a bed with catch-phrases and colloquialisms. From time to time it can even be seen walking arm-in-arm with Standard English. So what *is* a cliché?

Suffice it to say that the Bible is our guiding light: in the beginning was the Word, and the Word was with God, and the Word was God. As soon as that Word made a few friends the first cliché was born. Ever since then, on the principle that familiarity breeds contentment, we have turned to the cliché as a matter of course. It has been a rod and a staff to comfort us. It has been the *lingua franca* in a world of foreign bodies. It has been a welcoming, well-worn armchair for the universal bum. We are at ease with a cliché. Unhappily – to coin a phrase – we have taken it for granted.

The stereotype has always had a bad press. Consider these examples:

The cliché is a special effect that no longer comes off.

A trite or stereotyped phrase or expression; a hackneyed theme, plot or situation in fiction or drama.

There is no bigger peril either to thinking or education than the popular phrase.

A coin so battered as to be defaced.

A word or phrase that has lost much of its force through over-exposure; an idea, action or habit that has become trite through over-use.

Such are the cliché definitions of the cliché. How sharper than a serpent's tooth it is to have a thankless lexicographer! In his famous *Dictionary of Clichés*, the late, great Eric Partridge even talks about 'that excellent blood sport: cliché-hunting'. It is Vampirism. It is biting the hand that feeds us and then going for the neck.

The Finest Swordsman In All France has no truck with this carping criticism. Its flashing blade is raised in defence of the cliché. It celebrates the stereotype and hails the hackneyed phrase.

In its search for the best of the bunch and the cream of the crop, it explores every avenue and leaves no stone unturned. It gives the cliché its place in the sun. Using Alliteration's Artful Aid it allows the stereotype to savour the sweet smell of success. Without prejudice.

Clichés are everywhere. Culture is sustained by cliché concepts. Science proceeds by cliché methodology. Politics thrives on cliché attitudes. Industry operates on cliché assumptions. Education works within cliché traditions. Professions deal in cliché jargon. Christianity offers a cliché message. And the mass media reinforces all these clichés with its own cliché techniques. Attacking the cliché is thus gross self-abuse.

What, then, *is* a cliché?

A cliché is something which has earned our respect. It has given us yeoman service or it would not have achieved cliché-status. It is language with sweat on its brow and lines on its face. It is an idea with blisters on its hands. It is a course of action with mud on its boots. In short, a cliché is a veteran workman in danger of being made redundant. It is a symbol of honest toil. It is the salt of the earth.

Though found in abundance the cliché is an endangered species. In trying to protect it *The Finest Swordsman In All France* is giving it due reward for its labour and grateful thanks for its warm companionship.

Books

A novel which protests against the unrest and insincerity of modern life to-day, and at the same time makes a passionate plea for a simpler existence, lived close to nature, which shall lessen the importance of mere external possessions while emphasising the value of interior development . . .

The Centaur Algernon Blackwood. Blurb for Penguin edition, 1938.

The origin of the book is lost in the mists of time-travel. It has come a long way in six thousand years and its hieroglyphics have changed under the impress of mass-market publishing. It now knows that the cliché is the shortest distance between two bestsellers.

This section is in no way exhaustive. It simply wanders along some of the main thoroughfares of fiction and pickpockets shamelessly. Mindful of the opinion of Dickens – 'There are some books of which the backs and covers are the best part' – it does not neglect the title or the blurb. Plot and character also get due recognition and there are flavoursome extracts from a wide variety of sources.

Sacrifices have been inevitable. No room has been found for this piquant moment from *Stiletto* by Harold Robbins:

'Do not smile,' his uncle had snapped. 'In America, the Society is very important. Matteo is the richest man in all Sicily.'

And it has been necessary to omit this priceless exchange from *Unnatural Death* by Dorothy L Sayers:

'That's so. Well there's only one thing that could prevent

3

that happening, and that's – oh, lord! Do you know what it works out at? – The old, old story beloved of novelists – the missing heir!'

'Good lord, yes . . . you're right. Damn it all, what fools we were not to think of it before . . .'

Because children's fiction has had to be excluded from this study, this passage from the work of Captain Frank H. Shaw has gone:

The wrinkled old man with the slanting eyes laid a gnarled finger on an outspread map.

'That is the land I hate,' he said, with a suggestion of a snarl in his voice. His companion nodded and his already dark face grew darker.

'Britain – yes! I agree. I, too, have hated Britain since I first heard its accursed name. To-day I hate it more than ever. It has foiled my schemes for the universal brother-hood of mankind. I – ha, ha! – have beaten the invincible Britain once or twice, comrade, and I shall beat her again!'

And finally we must accord the tribute of a passing sigh to this speech from *In Maremma* by Ouida. The sole reason that it was not sent an invitation to appear here in person is that this anthology does not run to a section on Unreadable Victoriana.

'Such love!' said Sanctis, with an impetuosity not natural to him, and a passion of scorn for which all words were too poor and small. 'Have you never thought that it is your life you give away almost before it has begun? For you are so young: and this disgrace which you take upon you will last so long, so long; last till you lie in the grave, however old you be when death comes to you. Why should you give yourself to him? Why should you not be honestly loved in open day? Why should you taint yourself with guilt that is not yours? Who will look at you after years passed in the solitude of those caves with a felon? Who will ever believe in your innocence, if innocent you still be? You shut the doors of fate upon yourself. You turn your life of your own will into a stone. Nature has made you glorious gifts and you throw them all away like rotting leaves. Think not that I speak for myself. I am nothing to you. I know I never touch a fibre of your heart or fancy. In all likelihood you will never see my face again. I speak for you: it is for you I sorrow. Better would it be for you to love a man dead in his coffin, than to love one whom at any hour the law may snatch from you and send to fret his years away in the horror of the prisons . . .'

They don't write speeches like that any more! Absence makes the heart grow fonder: now for present delights . . .

Classics

If one cannot enjoy reading a book over and over again, there is no use in reading it at all.

Oscar Wilde.

A classic is a cliché writ large. The very qualities that lift a book above the common herd only inspire the common herdsmen to follow suit. A trail-blazer is an author with a pack of would-be authors on his heels. 'An immortal story' is one that will never die because there are so very many to keep it alive in perpetuity.

It has always been so with the novel. Robinson Crusoe was not alone on his island for long. Defoes began to arrive by the boatload until not a bare patch of sand was left unoccupied. Gulliver found crowds of holiday-makers ready to accompany him on his travels, and Tom Jones learned that the world was full of orphans like himself. Poor Moll Flanders, of course, has not been off her back since 1722!

Prototypes continued. The Austen Metro was a popular model, as was the Brontë Land Rover. Though the market was dominated by the Dickens Omnibus there was still a regular demand for the Thackeray Family Saloon and the Robert Louis Stevenson Convertible. Inevitably, there was protest when foreign imports began to claim a large share of the British Market. Russian Estates were the main dangers, though buyers were found for many French vehicles – for the Dumas Cavalier and the Hugo Hatchback of Notre Dame. It was a relief to be able to buy British again with the Anna Sewell Colt and the H G Wells Time Machine.

The cars roll off the assembly lines of a million typewriters. External features may vary but the engines are invariably standard models. Such vehicles are proven, roadworthy, comfortable to drive. Copying a classic is writing with the safety-belt clunked and clicked.

Welcome to the Motor Show of literature! Choose your model and drive down the broad highways of imagination. Here is the original, the startling, the unexpected – and all those other things that you have seen a thousand times before. Classics are cars of consequence. Buy one now!

Titles

War and Peace
Crime and Punishment
North and South
Pride and Prejudice
Treasure Island
Women in Love
Lost Horizon
Victory
Kidnapped
Great Expectations

Blurbs

One moment Random's fortune is riding high: the next he may be unlucky in love, the victim of the press-gang, shipwrecked, robbed or in line to mend his fortunes by marrying an heiress . . . Only to find at the next turn that he is penniless, thrown into a debtor's prison, to be rescued by a long-lost relative. The greatest surprise comes a little later . . . in the course of a trading voyage Random is made rich by a Spanish don who turns out to be his father!

Roderick Random Tobias Smollet. Everyman Paperback.

The profligate Earl of Rochester, the frenzied salvationist Solomon Eagle, the abominable undertaker Chowles and Judith Malmayns, the venal plague nurse, companions in iniquity, add a nightmare dimension to the adventures of dauntless Leonard Holt and the lovely Amabel in the stricken city. Dominating this spectacular story of love, greed, betrayal, abduction, conspiracy and revenge is the towering structure of old St Paul's . . . Cathedral . . . Public haunt of gallants and rogues . . . pest house . . . and blazing inferno.

Old St Paul's Harrison Ainsworth. Pan.

Murder, theft, rape, patricide, twisted passion . . .

Three Short Novels Dostoevsky. Bantam Classic.

The master thief Fagin, the sly, impish Artful Dodger, the murderer Bill Sikes and Nancy, one of the most famous victims in literature – all of them live forever in our minds. Wrapped in an unforgettable atmosphere of mystery and evil, sin and innocence, the famous scenes in *Oliver Twist* have lost none of their power to move and terrify.

Oliver Twist Charles Dickens. Fontana.

The story of three men who discovered a living legend in the heart of Africa . . . the beautiful white queen – mysterious, cruel, captivating, who ruled over a dark and savage people, and who held the secret of love, and the secret of life itself – She-Who-Must-Be-Obeyed.

She H Rider Haggard. Hodder paperback.

What makes a man forget his code of honour and register loyalty only to an evil cause? What makes a man turn against society, betray not only himself, but his dependants, his friends, his country? Fanaticism seems too thin a word to describe the process . . . We go to the dingy shop in the gloomy London street, and amid its shady wares discover Verloc, secret agent, Winnie his wife, and Stevie, her half-witted brother. From here we penetrate a little further to discover 'The Professor', Michaelis, ticket-of-leave man . . .

The Secret Agent Joseph Conrad. Everyman Paperback

He is one of the most attractive heroes in twentieth century fiction. Bennett, who believed inordinately in the interestingness of ordinary things and ordinary people, was never more successful in revealing the interestingness of an

apparently ordinary man than in ~~Edwin Clayhanger~~ ...

Clayhanger Arnold Bennett. Penguin.

Plots

Rags to riches.

Search for treasure, gold or diamond mines.

Search for mythical paradise or legendary whale.

Adventures on a desert island.

Dark deeds in Victorian underworld.

Saga that explores the major abstractions such as war, peace, life, death, love, art and God.

Naked passion that overcomes barriers of class, creed, colour and narrow social convention.

High romance set against the French Revolution, the American Civil War or the Great War.

Doubling ('Good heavens, the likeness is uncanny!') which enables a pauper to pass for a prince and a commoner to masquerade as a king.

Protest against Modern Life.

Characters

The trusty servant.

The mysterious benefactor.

Swashbuckling heroes in period costume.

Larger-than-life villains with giveaway names.

Comical clergymen.

9

The orphan, male or female, who undergoes the most dreadful trials and tribulations before being found to be of noble descent.

The embattled heroine who is trapped in a dismal existence on the Yorkshire Moors, in the wilds of Wessex, or on her husband's estate in the filthy Midlands.

The unlikely lovers whose antipathy towards each other is so strong that it can only end in marriage in the last chapter.

Guilt-ridden protagonists trying to expiate a crime or live down a tragic mistake in their past.

The silent lover, male or female, who lets the adored object exhaust all the other romantic possibilities before getting due reward at the altar for patience above and beyond the call of duty.

Text

'Who was it who took the obscure Amy Robsart, the daughter of an impoverished and dotard knight – the destined bride of a moonstruck, moping enthusiast, like Edmund Tressilian, from her lowly fates and held out to her in prospect, the brightest fortune in England, and perchance in Europe? Why, man, it was I – as I have often told thee – It was I who watched the wood while he beat for the deer – It was I who, to this day, am blamed by her family as the companion of her flight, and were I in their neighbourhood, would be fain to wear a shirt of better stuff than Holland linen, lest my ribs should be acquainted with Spanish steel. Who carried their letters? – I. Who amused the old knight and Tressilian? – I. Who planned their escape? – It was I. It was I, in short, Dick Varney, who pulled this pretty little daisy from its lowly nook, and placed it in the proudest bonnet in England.'

Kenilworth Walter Scott.

'That does not surprise me,' said Mr Garland, 'it is a natural consequence of the events you have recalled; of this dreary time and place; and above all, of this wild and dismal night. A dismal night indeed! Hark! How the wind is howling!'

The Old Curiosity Shop Charles Dickens.

'Of all the people on earth, you least expected to see me?' she said.

'I could not believe it to be you. I can scarcely believe it now. You are not' – the apprehension came suddenly into his mind – 'a prisoner?'

'No. I am accidentally possessed of a power over one of the keepers here . . .'

A Tale of Two Cities Charles Dickens.

'Papa, what is he going to do? Is there any – any *danger*?

'To me, you mean?' She nodded. 'Yes, I suppose there is danger to me. Yes. But tell me, is there danger to *you*? Are you in love with my persecutor, Mr Bold?'

She stood silent for a moment, then, as she ran from the room, she murmured, 'Yes'.

The Warden Anthony Trollope.

'Barbara! Barbara!' he ejaculated, 'I have seen Thorn . . . Every drop of blood within me began to tingle, and an impulse came upon me to spring upon him and accuse him of the murder of Hallijohn,' went on Richard in the same excited manner. 'But I restrained it; perhaps my courage failed. One of the reproaches against me used to be that I was a physical coward, you know, Barbara,' he added, his tone changing to bitterness. 'In a struggle Thorn would have had the best of it; he is taller and more powerful than I, and might have battered me to death. A man who can commit one murder won't hesitate at a second.'

East Lynne Mrs Henry Wood.

His unreasonable anger terrified her, and she glided from him, without obviously moving, as she said, 'I am only a girl – do not speak to me so!'

'All the time you knew – how very well you knew – that your new freak was my misery. Dazzled by brass and scarlet – O, Bathsheba – this is woman's folly indeed!'

Far from the Madding Crowd Thomas Hardy.

'Suddenly he caught hold of my neck. Damn him! I hit him. I hit him without looking. "Won't you save your own life – you infernal coward?" he sobs. Coward! He called me an infernal coward! Ha! ha! ha! ha! He called me – ha! ha! ha! . . .'

He had thrown himself back and was shaking with laughter. I had never in my life heard anything so bitter as that noise.

Lord Jim Joseph Conrad.

His body vibrated taut and powerful as he closed upon her and crushed her, breathless and dazed and destroyed, crushed her upon his breast. Ah, it was terrible, and perfect . . .

Women in Love D H Lawrence.

'Henry Lakington is the second most dangerous man in London.'

Bulldog Drummond Sapper.

Crime

'Also, he's a big bastard. I wouldn't want ever to tangle with him. This guy chews railroad spikes and spits out carpet tacks.' He paused. 'Pardon the cliché,' he said. He pronounced it 'cleesh'.

'Til Death Ed McBain.

Crime does not pay overmuch attention to complexity of character, to subtle loveplay between form and content, or to the felicities of the mandarin style. It has other things on its mind.

Whether written by dons or doctors, cops or criminals, Lords, Ladies or Gentlemen, the crime novel belongs to the literature of sensation. It is a million dollars beckoning from a bank vault. A rotten precinct waiting to be cleaned up. A body in the library hoping for a Silver Dagger Award.

Detective fiction is as distinctive as Wedgwood pottery. Plot is paramount, characterisation minimal, murder obligatory, clues abundant, red herrings optional, puzzle value high. An enclosed setting is vital. Whodunnit? Motives are handed out like party hats then the detective, male or female, but always the central character, ties up all the loose ends in a revelation speech.

Modern crime novels play to slightly different rules but the refereeing is just as strict as before. Plot is subservient to character, which develops under the pressure of events. Murder is no longer the standard crime. Realism and gruesome detail intrude. Clues are peripheral. The leisurely gait of the old-style whodunnit is replaced by the hectic pace of the thriller. Pat solutions perish. The central character is never a brilliant detective who, by the sheer power of deductive reasoning, succeeds where the baffled officers of the law have failed. Crime is no longer a parlour game for advanced intellects. It is nasty, brutish and short on sentiment.

From super sleuths to hard-boiled cops, from poisoned husbands to dismembered corpses, from country houses to Californian skylines, crime-writing pays dividends with unlimited clichés.

Titles

Blue Murder
Sudden Death
Kill with Kindness
Blood Runs Cold
Guilty as Hell
Unwanted Corpse
Trouble is My Business
Violence is Golden
Dead Men Don't Talk
Cop Killer

Blurbs

Into his telephone breathe the husky, sultry voices of movie stars, the slurred accents of gangsters, the prim tones of small-town girls, the clipped phrases of the police . . .

The Little Sister Raymond Chandler. Penguin.

'The prisoner had the means – the arsenic. She had the expert knowledge, and she had the opportunity to administer it.' The judge's summing-up was clear. Harriet Vane was guilty. And Harriet Vane should hang. But the jury disagreed . . .

Strong Poison Dorothy L Sayers. Four Square.

He moves fast, he shoots straight. A blunt instrument of justice, he copes with trouble by walking right into it. But the priceless Maltese Falcon and the lovely Miss Wonderly are man-traps for the fleetest human game . . .

The Maltese Falcon Dashiell Hammett. Penguin.

Mike is found in the gutter – an alcoholic on the verge of losing his mind. It has taken him seven years to reach this point – seven years of guilt believing he has caused the death of Velda, the girl he loved. Then he hears: Velda may still be alive, but before he can be sure, he must find and destroy a master killer called the Dragon.

Mike Hammer versus the Dragon – care to take odds on the result . . .?

The Girl Hunters Mickey Spillane. Corgi.

Plots

The perfect murder.

Sensational bank robbery or heist.

Mafiadrama in a Godfathery vein.

Jack the Ripper.

Terrorist hijacking.

Skullduggery in boxing or horse-racing.

Drug racket smashed by undercover agent.

Escaped prisoner bent on revenge.

Man versus the multi-national ('Corporate corruption exposed by the one man they could not buy').

Mayhem in the Middle East with oily Arabs, today's equivalent of sinister Orientals.

A community terrorised ('He's killed fifty-one times, Lieutenant, and he'll kill again') by a homicidal maniac.

Mysterious disappearance of wife, husband, lover, child, diplomat, physicist, heir to a vast fortune, witness for the prosecution, Prime Minister, President of the United States, or compromising photographs.

Characters

The perfect murderer.

The fallible and human-like-the-rest-of-us sleuth.

Authority figure with criminal son.

The female killer, more deadly than the male.

The heavy or hit-man.

The unseen Mr Big, who pulls the strings.

The tough cop ('Quit stalling, wise guy, or I'll break your other goddam leg!') with brutal interviewing techniques.

Comical servants, taxi drivers, barmaids, village bobbies and Gawd-bless-you-Guv'nor newsvendors.

The ordinary man caught up in a frightening web of intrigue, corruption and murder.

The unidentified corpse.

The investigative journalist who stumbles onto something bigger and nastier than he ever imagined.

Red herrings and disposable victims.

Text

'Well, Jack, we was a-openin' this here grave, which is Lady Thorpe's grave what died last New Year's Day, for to be ready for her 'usband's body, see, what's to be buried to-morrow. We begins to shovel away the earth, one at each end, like, and we hadn't got much more than a foot or so below ground level, as you might say, when Dick drives his spade down a good spit, and he says to me, "Dad," he says, "there's something in here." And I says to him, "What's that?" I says, "what do you mean? Something in here?" and then I strike my spade down hard

16

and I feels something sort of between soft and hard, like, and I says, "Dick," I says, "that's a funny thing, there *is* something here . . ." '

The Nine Tailors Dorothy L Sayers.

Della Street, Perry Mason's confidential secretary, laid an expensively engraved visiting-card on the lawyer's desk.

Mason looked at it, said: 'Mrs Summerfield Malden. What does *she* want, Della?'

'Does the name mean anything to you?' Della Street asked.

'No. Should it?'

She nodded. 'It's been in the newspapers. She's Steffanie Malden, the wife, or rather, the widow of Dr Summerfield Malden. Dr Malden was flying his own plane to a medical convention in Salt Lake City. The plane crashed.

'Yesterday's paper had the story. It was spotted from the air within less than an hour of the time it crashed. It was on one of the dry lakes in the desert. Dr Malden's charred body was found in it. Apparently, he'd had trouble, had tried to make a forced landing and had crashed.'

Mason nodded. 'I remember now. Dr Malden was noted as a surgeon, wasn't he . . .?'

The Case of the Fugitive Nurse Erle Stanley Gardner.

George nodded. 'I suppose they'll hang me,' he said. 'You know, I'm not afraid. I've been awfully lonely all my life.'

'Now don't talk like that,' the detective returned, looking at him sharply. 'While there's life, there's hope, you know. You don't have to get depressed.'

'Oh, I'm not depressed,' George returned, 'I'm really quite happy now.'

A moment later the car took him away to meet his destiny.

More Deadly than the Male James Hadley Chase.

'You see,' said Miss Marple, 'once Mark and Josie knew that you were going to make a new will, they'd *have* to do something. They'd already committed *two* murders on account of the money. So they might as well commit a third . . . Any doctor would think death from heart trouble quite natural in the circumstances. Josie had loosened one of the stone balls on the balcony and she was going to let it crash down afterwards. His death would be put down to the shock of the noise.'

Melchett said: 'Ingenious devil.'

The Body in the Library Agatha Christie.

'Very well, Mr Marlowe. I'm ready to call the police now. But I don't think you'll like it. I don't think you'll like it at all.'

'Why?'

'Because there's murder in it, Mr Marlowe, and murder is a very nasty word – don't you think?'

'Come on up,' I said. 'I'll wait.'

I hung up. I got the bottle of Old Forester out. There was nothing slow about the way I poured myself a drink and dropped it down my throat.

The Little Sister Raymond Chandler.

Horror

The last man alive sat all alone in his house. Suddenly, the front door bell rang . . .

Horror goes back to ancient myth, legend and folklore but its more immediate roots are in the soil of the Gothic novel. It is rich, fertile, well-harrowed soil with a top-dressing of terror. Blood flows freely in its furrows and vermin feed off its crop.

Gothic novelists threw in the lot – rape, incest, murder, magic, diabolism, bestiality, ghosts, poltergeists and predatory animals. Long after their original publication, the unholy trinity of *Frankenstein, Dr Jekyll and Mr Hyde* and *Dracula* haunted the writing of the horror story and went on to receive the supreme accolade of meeting the stars of Hollywood.

Today's spine-chillers are of a different order. Foul deeds are no longer signposted by foul weather. Graveyards are safer places and the lonely laboratory has been annexed by the National Health Service. Ghosts have matured. Chains rarely clank, spectres seldom walk through walls, skulls do not glow in the dark and bleeding hands do not bar the way to the forbidden chamber. When strange moaning noises are heard at midnight, they usually come from the heroine as she is being pleasured on the fourposter by the chauffeur.

Old traditions are still honoured but some of the more cumbersome apparatus has been junked. The ordinary has ousted the extraordinary. Commonplace settings are the current cliché. Instead of being announced by a deafening fanfare of sensational effects, terror arises where least expected – on a train, in a park, up a ladder, down a street, along a canal bank. And in broad daylight! The unknown emerges from the known and loved and trusted.

In Ira Levin's *Rosemary's Baby* the longed-for child becomes the object of fear when its parents believe it is destined for witchcraft. In William Peter Blatty's *The Exorcist*, a young girl is possessed. Stephen King's *The Shining* shows a congenial father turned into an axe-wielding monster. Horror has subverted hearth and home. There is no safe place to hide any more.

Titles

Black Mass
Curse of Dracula
Force of Darkness
Tomb of Frankenstein
The Masque of the Red Death
Bride of Satan
Fangs of the Wolf Man
Blood in the Crypt
Devil Creature
Danse Macabre
Omen
Witching Hour

Blurbs

Sir Gifford Hillary returns from the grave – now accused of murder.

'Killed' by one of his wife's lovers, he became a Ka, unseen but seeing all.

Plot and counterplot, ruse and subterfuge, lead through a story of extraordinary fascination and excitement: a story which seems at first fantastic but is later seen to be entirely logical.

The Ka of Gifford Hillary Dennis Wheatley. Arrow.

The immortal horror story of a monster fashioned by a man and the curse of death and destruction wrought by its creation. Victor Frankenstein, a young Swiss student of the natural sciences . . . creates a huge, hideous creature which, scorned by everyone because of its ugliness, vows to spend the rest of its life seeking revenge against the human race.

Frankenstein Mary Shelley. Dell Paperback.

They were padding up the stairs, growling, jostling for position. Mandersby stared at the slowly opening door with dilated eyes. He could see two amber specks of light advancing towards the bed. Suddenly there was a weight upon his legs, and the outline of a gaunt head with gaping jaws. Then a tongue – cold as death – upon his cheek . . .

15th Fontana Book of Great Ghost Stories Selected by
R Chetwynd-Hayes.

London – a city haunted by its violent past . . . tortures in the Tower . . . massacres at Tyburn . . . gaslit murders in Victorian parlours . . . centuries of timeless terror.

The walking corpse of Piccadilly – the demon lover of Kensington – the death-watcher of Highgate – the spectral chimes of Marylebone – the Pimlico bones – the horror-house by the Thames.

Chilling tales of ghosts and ghouls, mystery and madness . . .

London Tales of Terror Ed. Jacqueline Visick. Fontana.

Plots

Man versus the Monster he has created.

The vampire myth.

Imprisonment in a haunted house.

Satanism.

Exorcism.

Dualism in the Jekyll and Hyde tradition.

A series of horrific crimes by a bestial killer.

The Un-dead at work.

The remote island with weird, malevolent life-forms.

Guilty conscience drives man to suicide.

Re-enactment of a murder from long ago.

A family bearing a tragic curse.

Characters

The Mad Doctor.

Dracula or his descendants.

Monsters.

Ghosts and ghoulies.

Children possessed by the Devil.

The sceptic who refuses to believe in ghosts and who is their first victim.

The beautiful young girl victim-figure.

The innocent person caught up in witchcraft.

The strange old woman with psychic powers.

Sinister servants.

The visitor at the mercy of weird relatives.

Animals that turn on humans.

The telepathist who is warned of horrors to come.

The body-snatchers who get a shock.

The creepy vicar.

Text

The monk beheld her with anxious curiosity. Suddenly she

uttered a long and piercing shriek. She appeared to be seized with an excess of delirium; she tore her hair, beat her bosom, used the most frantic gestures, and drawing the poniard from her girdle, plunged it into her left arm. The blood gushed out plentifully; and as she stood on the brink of the circle, she took care that it should fall on the outside. The flames retired from the spot on which the blood was pouring. A volume of dark clouds rose slowly from the ensanguined earth, and ascended gradually till it reached the vault of the cavern. At the same time, a clap of thunder was heard, the echo pealed fearfully along the subterranean passages, and the ground shook beneath the feet of the enchantress . . .

The Monk Matthew Lewis.

The most racking pangs succeeded: a grinding in the bones, deadly nausea, and a horror of the spirit that cannot be exceeded at the hour of birth or death. Then these agonies began swiftly to subside, and I came to myself as if out of a great sickness. There was something indescribably new, and, from its very novelty, incredibly sweet. I felt younger, lighter, happier in body; within I was conscious of a heady recklessness, a current of disordered sensual images running like a mill race in my fancy, a solution of the bonds of obligation, an unknown but not an innocent freedom of the soul. I knew myself, at the first breath of this new life, to be more wicked, tenfold more wicked, sold a slave to original evil . . .

The Strange Case of Dr Jekyll and Mr Hyde R L Stevenson.

'Ollendorffian beggar!' said Montgomery. 'You'll bleed and weep if you don't look out.'

'He has five fingers; he is a five-man like me,' said the Ape Man . . .

It was on our way back that we came upon the dead rabbit. The red body of the wretched little beast was rent to pieces, many of the ribs stripped white, and the backbone indisputably gnawed.

At that Montgomery stopped. 'Good God!' said he, stooping down and picking up some of the crushed vertebrae to examine them more closely. 'Good God!' he repeated, 'what can this mean?'

'Some carnivore of yours has remembered its old habits,' I

said, after a pause. 'This backbone has been bitten through.'

He stood staring at it, with his face white and his lip pulled askew. 'I don't like this,' he said slowly . . .

The Island of Doctor Moreau H G Wells.

'. . . this house had a bad reputation long before you came to live here. There was some talk of a murder committed here way back in the last century. Instead of ranting at the girl, you should try to help her.'

Mrs Fortesque gave the impression she might faint if given the least encouragement, while her husband sank into a chair and murmured:

'This is all beyond me. Are you saying that my daughter can see spooks?'

'I'm saying that she is aware of a phenomenon that cannot be explained in mundane terms. She has an affinity with the past and possibly an unconscious ability to give substance to – for want of a better expression – a personality extension. Something that is trapped in a haunting pattern.'

'Good God, woman, you must be mad!'

'Madness is the sanity shared by the few . . .'

The Hanging Tree R Chetwynd-Hayes.

I feel that the time has come when I must endeavour to face facts. These past few nights I have been frightened – scared stiff – really terrified. Ten months ago I was a sane, strong, healthy man; now I am weak, irresolute and, I fear, on the verge of going mad. Perhaps I am only imagining things . . .

The Haunting of Toby Jugg Dennis Wheatley.

Romance

Love is the greatest and most irresistible force in the world – and our hope of heaven.

Barbara Cartland

Of all the genres romantic fiction is the most spoof-proof. It has remained faithfully wedded to its formulas and its critics have been swept aside by the sheer relentlessness of its clichés. Written almost exclusively by – and for – women, it has wooed and won its share of the market and kept it in a firm embrace. Since it is its own best parody it defies cynics and satirists alike.

Its escapism is impregnable.

A basic tenet of romantic fiction is that the author's name, real or pseudonymous, should sound like a character from the book – Lucille Andrews, Elizabeth Cadell, Bess Norton, Margaret Mayo, Jean Ure, Susan Alexander, Rosemary Pollock, Stephanie Kincaid, Sally Wentworth . . . What reader would be tempted to make a journey to romance with an author named Kurt Vonnegut Jnr or Vladimir Nabokov or Anais Nin? The name of the game is the name-game.

Plot and character dictate a house style that is breathless, melodramatic and honeyed. Students of punctuation will know that the romantic novelist favours the exclamation mark and the dash. Since protest and uncertainty lie at the heart of the archetypal story, the novel is often a forest of exclamation marks surrounded by miles of fencing. Like the protagonists themselves, the punctuation moves from the vertical to the horizontal. The treasured three dots must not be forgotten. Skilled practitioners can use dashes and dots with such precision that their prose has a sub-text in morse code.

But it is the element of romance that attracts the reader. Romantic literature is a fantasy world in which rugged heroes survive danger and deception to claim melting heroines in their strong arms. It's about forbidden yearnings and precious moments and promises by moonlight. It's about faraway places with strange-sounding names, faraway over the sea. It's about a search for love, for light, for life, for hope. It's the biggest cliché of them all – a glimpse of heaven in a mass-market paperback.

Titles

Loving
Now and Forever
Season of Passion
The Enchanted Heart
Sweet Adventure
The Midnight Embrace
Tender Longings
Hold Me Forever
Forbidden Yearnings
Where is Love?

Blurbs

Daphne Fields is known to millions and loved by millions. Her novels turn pain into joy, give her readers hope and the promise of new love when tears blind them. Her stories are drawn from her own struggle to choose between two men . . . to choose between being a mother, an artist, a lover.

Once In a Lifetime Danielle Steel. Sphere.

If you've been at the office all day come with us to Barbados tonight. Pick up any Silhouette romance and come with us on a journey to love in beautiful, faraway places . . .

Advertisement for Silhouette Romances.

It was a terrible shock to Aldona when the disagreeable Lionel Downs told her bluntly that he had caught her father

embezzling his employers – and if she didn't want him to go to prison she had better do as Lionel suggested and go with him on holiday to Malta. What could she do but comply?

Price to be Met Jessica Steele. Mills and Boon.

A stormy panorama of passion and grief . . . A uniquely moving story that spans generations . . . A backcloth that stretches from Australia to the Vatican, from New Zealand to London . . .

The Thorn Birds Colleen McCullough. Futura.

Plots

The holiday romance.

The hospital romance.

The Regency romance.

The Restoration romance.

The eternal triangle.

The disastrous marriage.

The forbidden fruit.

Attraction of opposites.

The world-wide search for a lasting relationship.

Love in a blue lagoon, at a rendezvous in Athens, or at some other Garden of Eden into which the harsh realities of the world do not intrude.

Burning passions leaving bitter harvests.

The power of love to ennoble the most wicked and despicable human beings and to enrich their lives.

28

Characters

The man or woman who goes on holiday to get over a broken romance and who meets someone else there.

The new night nurse who has both doctors and patients in hot pursuit.

The heroine in historical costume who is at the mercy of all the rakes in London until saved from a fate worse than death by the handsome hero.

The tortured man forced to choose between wife and mistress but unable to give either of them up.

The girl from the city who stays in the country and learns about the primitive animal passions of nature red in tooth and claw.

The widow or widower who believes that love is a thing of the past until some enchanted evening, when they may see a stranger . . .

The ambitious secretary who uses her charms to get on then finds she is trapped by love into an unsuitable relationship with her boss.

The best friend on whose shoulder they can cry.

The heroine trapped by circumstance and forced to accept a Corrupt Bargain ('I'll close my eyes to that if you open your legs to this') with the villain in order to protect someone she loves.

The guilt-ridden man or woman who falls madly in love with someone very much younger than themselves.

The man or woman who loses himself or herself in work to the exclusion of all else and then finds, when the top of the tree has been reached, that it is lonely up there without someone to love.

Awkward relatives, jealous rivals, rapacious bosses, office wolves and other hindrances.

Text

He drew her scarce-resisting head downward to the pillow

beside his own, and leaned his brow, unchidden, against her wet cheek. Her lips were quivering with sobs; she could not speak, but her soul was deeply glad. What mattered his weakness, his shrinking, his shyness now? What cared she that the fleshly garb of the poet wore blue spectacles and – had now but one arm! Beneath it all throbbed the mighty heart of a hero, and that heart was hers.

Myrtle's Hero Jennie Chappell. (Victorian novelette)

He was lifting her off her feet, carrying her to the divan, his fingers trembling over the fastening of her robe which was discarded with an impatient haste, baring her body to the hunger of his gaze.

'Aren't you going to kiss me?' she asked innocently.

A hectic flush lay along his high cheekbones, his eyes glittering beneath the thick lashes. His body seemed to burn against hers as he flung off his own robe.

'Danielle.'

It was the hoarse plea of a man who has reached the limits of endurance and prays that he will not be pushed past it . . .

Daughter of Hassan Penny Jordan.

'I fell . . . don't know – how – quite . . . it wasn't . . . purposely, Peter.'

'I know.'

And then – 'It's better than having – to – go on – living – all alone . . . isn't it?' and as he could not answer she said with a note of fear in her voice –

'Do you think it . . . will be very – lonely?'

'My arms will hold you all the way, beloved -- just as my heart will hold you for ever.'

She gave a little sigh of contentment and tried to move her head nearer to him but even as he moved his arm to help her, she was gone . . .

But the birds still sang in the garden outside.

Than This World Dreams Of Ruby M Ayres.

'Why, you – you – you –'

She stammered helplessly, beating at his chest with harmless fists. But soon she was laughing, too, overwhelmed with his love and the depths he had gone to for her.

30

He kissed her, and the moment grew magically between them. He picked her up in his arms and looked down into her glowing face.

'You're mine, darling. You're my wife, Jan. After all this time, you're really mine.'

Their kisses grew into a rushing fire of passion that swept them away into a world of new and lasting love.

The Fires of Passion Arlene Hale.

There was an elation in Larina's voice that was very moving, and as she looked up at Wynstan she saw tears in his eyes – but they were tears of joy.

'He kept his . . . promise! Only I did not . . . realise that it was he bringing me . . . life and . . . light.'

'That is what he found himself,' said Wynstan, in his deep voice.

'I understand you,' Larina said, 'and I think . . . he must have . . . sent you to me.'

'I am sure he did but why did you run away?'

She hid her face against him and whispered:

'I am . . . so ashamed . . . of what I . . . suggested.'

Wystan's arms tightened as she went on:

'I am not . . . really sure . . . about what men and women . . . do when they . . . make love . . . but it must be . . . wonderful . . .'

No Time for Love Barbara Cartland.

31

Science Fiction

The whole creature heaved and pulsated convulsively. A lank tentacular appendage gripped the edge of the cylinder, another swayed in the air. Those who have never seen a living Martian can scarcely imagine the strange horror of its appearance . . .

The War of the Worlds H G Wells

Hunting for clichés in science fiction is like searching for salt water in the Pacific. They are elemental to the genre. As soon as a new and original concept is fashioned, it is pounced on and popularised until it is just another stereotype. The literature of the unknown is full of the familiar.

Science fiction is a Hackneyed carriage from which almost everyone has tried to thumb a lift – satirists, surrealists, social commentators, madmen, missionaries, cartoonists, fantasists, farceurs, propagandists, pornographers and prophets of doom. Yet its essence survives. It is a Tale of Wonder to keep the reader's mouth agape. An Astounding Story that disturbs scientifically. A double-glazed window on Another World.

Catastrophe is part of its staple diet. Among the terrors that SF writers have inflicted upon our planet are drought, flood, fire, snow, civil war, super-beasts, invaders from outer space, disease, general insanity, nuclear devastation and a wind from nowhere, a hurricane that blasted around the globe at hundreds of miles an hour. The disasters that have been dreamed up make the Plagues of Egypt look like so many eccentric conjuring tricks.

Science fiction has its shortcomings. It is very prodigal with its material, running too far, too fast, too frequently. The cliché jargon – cyborg, hyperspace, forcefield, transmogrifier, tempunauts and so on – does often clutter and confuse.

Characterisation is often no more than the selection of a name, sex and function. The prevailing house-style tends towards the hectic and the hyperbolic. And there is an underlying pessimism that points to a bleak future.

Nevertheless, it is one of the most entertaining and vigorous genres. SF is a questing, questioning mode. It is a literature of extremes but its heart is firmly in the right place. It is the end of civilisation as we know it – with a million sequels to come.

Titles

Moonbeast
Invaders in Space
The Time Mercenaries
Neutron Star
Stowaway to Mars
Voyage to Venus
Captive Universe
The Naked Sun
Strangers from Earth
After Doomsday

Blurbs

Colossus – the name of the super-computer as big as a large town, buried somewhere in the Rocky Mountains, now the sole arbiter of war and peace. But when the Russians produced a counterpart, the two computers seemed to have minds of their own!

Colossus D F Jones. Pan.

1984 had come and gone but there were still revolutionaries dedicated to the overthrow of the Syndicalist Government. And like all totalitarian governments, that of 2006 needed a secure prison for its really dangerous opponents. They found it, not in a remote area of the world, known or unknown, not in a distant galaxy, a spaceship's voyage away, but beyond all the limits known to man, a billion years in the past.

Hawksbill Station Robert Silverberg. Tandem.

For eight thousand years he had been a corpse drifting in space until the Martians revived him by the science of anti-mortics and told him: 'Earth is yours.' But how could anyone own a planet ravaged by atomic wars and peopled by mutants?

The Man who Owned the World Charles Eric Maine. Panther.

Plots

The conquest of space.

First contact with alien life-forms.

Robots and Androids.

Man versus the Machine.

Inner Space.

Time Travel.

Utopianism.

Alternative Universes.

After the Holocaust.

Immortality.

Future Sex.

Inter-galactic war.

Characters

The Mad Scientist.

Monsters from Outer Space.

Mutants.

34

Shape-changing aliens ('I think you should know, Captain, that one of us aboard this starship is not human!')

Lovable robots and Androids who are almost more-human-than-humans.

The omniscient guru figure who acts as mentor to the young hero.

Amazons and freak females.

The ordinary man who somehow manages to triumph against the best-laid plans of high technology.

Rulers of galactic empires who are corrupted by power and overreach themselves.

Romeo and Juliet look-alikes whose love life is complicated because the planets on which they live are at war with each other.

The Time Lord.

The superior alien who is feared by mankind at first but whose knowledge saves it from total destruction.

Strange children.

Lotus-eaters in a doomed society.

Text

It all began so suddenly. The reptilian forces of Megenth, long quiescent, suddenly began to expand due to the serum given them by Charles Engstrom, the power-crazed telepath. Jon Westerley was hastily recalled from his secret mission to Angos II. Westerley had the supreme misfortune of materialising within a ring of Black Force, due to the inadvertent treachery of Ocpetis Marn, his faithful Mnerian companion, who had, unknown to Westerley, been trapped in the Hall of Floating Mirrors, and his mind taken over by the renegade Santhis, leader of the Entropy Guild. That was the end of Westerley, and the beginning of the end for us.

Zirn Left Unguarded . . . Robert Sheckley.

A figure was lying on the gravel, chest downwards, but with the head turned to show one side of its face. The first glance at it showed me the bright red streak across the cheek.

'Stop!' I shouted at her.

There was enough alarm in my voice to check her.

I had spotted the triffid now. It was lurking among the bushes, well within striking range of the sprawled figure.

'Back! Quick!' I said.

Still looking at the man on the ground, she hesitated.

'But I must –' she began, turning towards me. Then she stopped. Her eyes widened, and she screamed.

I whipped round to find a triffid towering only a few feet behind me . . .

The Day of the Triffids John Wyndham.

'By making a point 0100 turn we shall miss the storm by seven light weeks. I admit it is an appalling sharp curve, but I feel we should have at least that much leeway.'

She turned and stared at Maltby. 'Prepare yourself. At half a light year a minute even a hundredth of a degree turn makes some people black out.'

'Not me,' said Maltby, and tensed his Dellian muscles.

She fainted three times during the next four minutes as he sat there watching her. But each time she came to within seconds.

'We human beings,' she said wanly, finally, 'are a poor lot. But at least we know how to endure.'

The terrible minutes dragged. And dragged. Maltby began to feel the strain of that infinitesimal turn. He thought at last! How could these people ever hope to survive a direct hit on a storm?

Abruptly, it was over; a man's voice said quietly: 'We have followed the prescribed course, noble lady, and are now out of dang –'

He broke off with a shout . . .

The Storm A E van Vogt.

'. . . YET OVER all did Thongor triumph, for the Immortal Gods themselves were leagued with him in war against the Dark Ones. Armed with the very lightnings of Heaven, Thongor the Mighty broke asunder the black bastions of Zaar and the ancient City of Magicians, with all its evil wisdom and dark science, sank beneath the waves of the unconquerable sea and was gone forever from the knowledge of men. And thus did the worshippers of the Third Lord of Chaos perish utterly from the earth, and thus shall the Servants of Darkness ever fail and fall, in whatever age or land they strive to dominate . . . for is it not written in *The Scarlet Edda* that Light shall forever be victorious against the Dark?'

– The Lemurian Chronicles

Thongor in the City of Magicians Lin Carter.

. . . Moving toward the centre of the lawn to catch the failing light, he read:

    Always keep up appearances.
    Always be doing something.
    Always be first or last.
    Always be alone.
    Always have a route of escape.
    Never hesitate, or you're lost.
    Never do anything odd – it wouldn't be noticed.
    Never move things – it makes gaps.
    Never touch anyone – DANGER! MACHINERY!
    Never run – they're faster.
    Never look at a stranger – it might be one of them.
    Some animals are really alive.

    Carr looked over his shoulder at the boarded-up house. A lean bird skimmed behind the roof. Somewhere down the block footsteps were clicking on concrete . . .

You're All Alone Fritz Leiber.

War

My argument is that War makes rattling good history; but Peace is poor reading.

The Dynasts Thomas Hardy.

War wins readers. Chronicles of combat and tales of heroism among the soldiery have been written for thousands of years. The perspective may have changed with time but the material has remained much the same. Livy still lives. He is now working on the sequel to *Horatius at the Bridge Too Far over the River Kwai*.

Henri Barbusse's *Under Fire* was the first of many pacifist novels to come out of the Great War. Similar in style, tone and structure was Erich Maria Remarque's influential *All Quiet On The Western Front*. France and Germany set the pattern. Barbusse's plot and Remarque's types have been enlisted by almost every army and are now battle-hardened veterans. Clichés know no boundaries.

The Second World War sent a new generation scurrying to its typewriters. An early classic was *The Naked and the Dead*. American youth versus the yellow men of Nippon. Ordinary guys caught up in the viciousness of war and suffering from fear, ignorance, injury and the stupidity of their officers. Death always on hand. Blood and irony. Mailer had nothing new to say about war itself but he had a tougher, louder and more frank way of saying it. For the Tell-It-Like-It-Was School, this book is basic training.

Sea and sky each provide a spacious canvas and authors have been generous with primary colours. Danger rides on or below the waves, and somewhere in England a grizzled martinet of an Air Chief Marshall demands a new bomb that will take the length of a novel to make, bounce on water and play the Dam Busters' March on impact.

For those who wish to write about land, sea *and* air forces, there is a hold-all on the market that carries the three of them. The POW Camp. In this cliché microcosm of humanity, anything goes – then goes again – then goes again and again . . .

The war story is a place to meet old friends rather than enemies.

Titles

Battle Cry
Bomber
Blitzkrieg
Convoy to Hell
Assignment: Gestapo
Alamein Attack
Spearhead General
Take or Destroy
Fields of Fire
Dawn Raid

Blurbs

Leutnant Micki Boden had been looking forward to some leave when his plane crash-landed and he found himself flung into the midst of the North African Campaign. Stranded in the heart of the Tunisian desert, Boden faced his toughest assignment yet: to support Rommel against the Allied Eighth Army.

But first he had to reach Rommel – in a captured Panzer tank carrying a wounded crew . . .

Panzer Platoon: Support Rommel Gunther Lutz. Sphere.

Hemingway's first and worst war wound still smarts in this immediately gripping and justly famous novel of war, retreat, desertion, love and bereavement.

A Farewell to Arms Ernest Hemingway. Penguin.

After years together in bloody combat with the Nazis, the cruiser's crew will disperse to fight in other ships, in other seas. But a call to *Andromeda's* youthful captain, Richard Blake, VC, changes everything. He puts to sea immediately. His mission: to seek out and destroy the raider.

And in this conflict, one ship must die.

A Ship Must Die Douglas Reeman. Arrow.

The sky around him was an inferno of darting flames and hurtling metal. Suddenly a blinding sheet of flame leapt from the engine and he throttled back with frantic haste. He knew it was only a matter of seconds before the whole plane ignited . . .

Biggles Learns to Fly Captain W E Johns. Armada.

Plots

A squad of men from wildly disparate backgrounds flung together in battle, meeting death and disillusion, emerging as true comrades.

Daring commando raid on impregnable target.

Thrilling escape from POW camp.

Convoy grapples with U-boat menace.

Enemy atrocities.

Battle of Britain.

Pearl Harbour.

Desert warfare.

The lost patrol in the Burmese jungle.

Sabotage of dangerous new enemy weapon.

Assassination attempt on Hitler, Churchill, General Eisenhower or others of high rank.

Victory on land, sea or air ('There's only one thing left to do now, Sergeant, and that's to pray') snatched from the jaws of defeat.

Characters

The reluctant hero.

The anti-hero with an ironic turn of phrase.

The mad general/group captain/naval captain.

Comical members of the lower ranks.

The grounded fighter pilot ('Put me back in the air, sir. Let me give Jerry some of his own medicine!').

The stoical leader who refuses to give in despite torture and humiliation in a POW camp.

The fixer who thrives on war and has an unlimited supply of booze, fags, nylon stockings and sexy women.

Inept officers who let their men down.

Hated enemies who endure a crisis together and become the best of friends.

American top brass in the I-can-shout-louder-and-curse-better-than-you tradition.

Prisoners or disgraced servicemen given a chance to redeem themselves on a mission impossible under a tough and sadistic leader.

Plucky wives, merry widows, doting mothers, loving daughters, luscious ladies of easy virtue, blondes in Operations Rooms, sexy female drivers of staff cars, obliging Wrens, beautiful nurses and other token women.

Text

Nobody could sleep. When morning came, assault craft would

be lowered and the first wave of troops would ride through the surf and charge ashore on the beach at Anopopei. All over the ship, all through the convoy, there was a knowledge that in a few hours some of them were going to be dead.

The Naked and the Dead Norman Mailer.

'Hello, Red Leader. Locust Control calling. Are you receiving me?'

'Hello, Locust Control. Red Leader answering. Receiving you loud and clear. Over.'

'Hello, Red Leader. Locust Control calling. Bandits five miles to port at angels two zero. Buster!'

'Hello, Locust Control. Red Leader answering . . .'

The war in the air. Standard issue.

Inside the walls, inside the cell-blocks, storey on storey, were cells for two thousand prisoners on capacity. Now, in the cells and in the passageways and in every nook and cranny lived some eight thousand men. English and Australian mostly – a few New Zealanders and Canadians – the remnants of the armed forces of the Far Eastern Campaign.

These men too were criminals. Their crime was vast. They had lost a war. And they had lived.

King Rat James Clavell.

The Hauptsturmführer brushed away a fly as it started to crawl across the blood-soaked bandage round his shoulder.

'Well, I'm still waiting.'

'We've been attached to the Herman Goerings.'

'Well I can't say you've done them much credit, whoever you are. On the East Front German soldiers expend all their ammunition before retreating; it's a lesson you don't take to heart, that's easy to see.'

The Fepo shepherded forward the rest of the Panzer crew; Spangel shook his head:

'I don't know these people, they look like deserters to me. They seem to have come to Africa thinking it was a good substitute for leave. Well, with our backs to the wall, that's a luxury the Third Reich can't afford. Kindly arrange to have them shot . . .'

Panzer Platoon: Support Rommel Gunther Lutz.

Someoné called for a stretcher-bearer, and through the tannoy a voice shouted, 'Damage control party port side forrard, at the double!'

Walker called, 'First lieutenant, sir!'

Blake took the telephone. 'Yes?'

'That shell passed through the starboard flag deck and exploded on the port side. Couple of boats are gone and the AA gun has been flung overboard.'

'Casualties?'

Blake winced as the hull bucked violently and he saw two great columns of water rise over the bridge before roaring down on the forecastle in a solid mass.

'The DCT is knocked out, sir. Guns is dead. About ten men in all. The doc's got some splinter cases aft . . .'

A Ship Must Die. Douglas Reeman.

Films

The origin of film is lost in the mists of time-lapse photography. Film is as old as the Beverly Hills and every bit as sun-kissed. From the first it has had a passionate affair with the cliché and their union has been blessed with progeny in abundance. Vast changes have taken place. There is a world of difference between the stock silent picture (Hero, Heroine, Mother, Villain, Vamp) and the multi-million dollar modern super-thriller like, say, *Octopussy* (Hero, Heroine, M, Villain, Vamp). Progress is progress.

This section cannot hope to do more than scratch at the surface of its subject. Unavoidably, there are gaps. Shortage of space has pushed out the Art Film, the Documentary, Social Realism, the Black Movie, the Musical, the Romance and the Ethnic Minority Film. And that enormous success – the Disaster Movie – has also had to be relegated to a mere mention. Those who feel deprived by the loss of these flourishing sub-cults should study a film like *The Proud Valley* (1939) which touches on all of them. Just count the clichés.

A lone giant of a man called David Goliath (Art Film symbolism) goes up the Welsh valleys during the Depression (Documentary) in search of work below ground beside blue-scarred miners (Social Realism). Because David Goliath is played by Paul Robeson (Black Movie) it is possible for him to fill the convenient hole in the bass section of the local choir (Musical). The valley town of Blaendy has its young hero, Owen, who is in love with a sharp-tongued but shapely girl (Romance). Welsh people (Ethnic Minority Film) are presented as salt-of-the-earth working class souls who put singing in the Blaendy Choir above anything. As a star in that choir, therefore, David Goliath is eased into a job at the mine without any difficulty. A serious Pit Accident occurs (Disaster Movie).

Apart from killing off a main caricature, Owen's father, the mine disaster closes off the new seams of coal. The pit is shut down. The whole town is out of work. Bitter boyos gather scraps of coal from the slag heaps and compare notes. It is a crisis situation. Owen's lady love flashes her eyes and puts her argument – 'We'll clear out of this poverty-stricken hole!' Though impressed by her tone – 'I like your spirit, love' – Owen cannot desert his mates. Accompanied by David, he leads a deputation on a long walk to London to confront the colliery owners. The march is a Jarrowing experience with montages of milestones and tramping feet. Being Welsh – 'They can't stop us singing' – the choir does its bit for well over two hundred miles.

Reaching London, they put their case with such fervour in a few short speeches that the owners reverse their decision. They accept the miners' claim that it is safe to reopen the seams blocked off by the disaster. Trouble below ground. David Goliath gives his life to save the pit. It returns to full productivity. The film ends with a shot of the mining landscape. Soaring above the full-throated choir, is the deep voice of Paul Robeson, dead but still in tune. Wales has found another St David.

The Proud Valley is in every sense a film made in black and white. Even the pathetic fallacy in its title is something of a cliché. Unable to deal with such a seminal film, this section nevertheless has rich seams of stereotypes. It sinks a number of shafts:

Comedies – 'It's all part of life's rich pageant.'

Cops and Robbers – 'What's the matter, Tony – getting yellow?'

Fantasy – 'Targ's gone berserk! He's taking the ship to Sansar . . . figures he can make peace with the Cylons . . .'

Historical Hokum – 'Fight, fight, fight! That's all you think of, Dick Plantagenet.'

Literature – 'I cannot live without my life . . . I cannot love without my soul . . .'

Spies – 'Of all the gin joints in all the towns in all the world, she walks into mine . . .'

Westerns – 'A man's gotta do what a man's gotta do.'

As for War Movies ('It's sheer murder to send a boy up there in a crate like that!'), they are another story. It is more than adequately told in the sub-sections above. Cameras are cannibals. Films feed off each other with companionable relish.

And now, let the motion picture industry speak for itself . . .

Publicity

Suppose the Devil was at the end of the forbidden path – Would you follow him?

Suppose your betrayer drove you to the depths – Would you make him pay?

The Forbidden Path (1918)

The mightiest dramatic spectacle of all the ages!

The Ten Commandments (1923)

A cast of 125,000!

Ben Hur (1927)

Oriental pride yields to Parisian kisses in a duel of male might and female charm . . . Exotic drama of love's sublime cruelty.

In Her Arms (1930)

He treated her rough – and she loved it!

Red Dust (1932)

The picture that kids the commissars!

Ninotchka (1937) – 'Don't pronounce it – see it!'

Each time they kissed . . . there was the thrill of love . . . the threat of murder!

Suspicion (1941)

From their darkened house on the corner they hurled

defiance at the town ... The sisters who lived up to the reputations they couldn't live down ...

The Guy Sisters (1042)

She knew strange fierce pleasures that no other woman could feel. She was one of the dreaded 'Cat People' — doomed to slink and prowl and court by night ... fearing always that a lover's kiss might change her into a snarling, clawing killer.

Cat People (1942)

Marilyn Monroe and 'Niagara' – a raging torrent of emotion that even nature can't control.

Niagara (1953)

Body of a boy! Mind of a monster! Soul of an unearthly thing!

I Was a Teenage Frankenstein (1957)

They touched and an evil spark was struck!

Portrait in Black (1960)

One man ... Three women ... One night!

The Night of the Iguana (1964)

If you miss the first five minutes you miss one suicide, two executions, one seduction and the key to the plot!

The Kremlin Letter (1970)

There's never been a movie like it!

Bugsy Malone (1976)

The most exciting original motion picture event of all time!

King Kong (1976)

Their love will arouse you
Their story will disturb you
The ending will startle you

The Sailor Who Fell from Grace with the Sea (1976)

50

Just when you thought it was safe to go back in the water . . .

Jaws 2 (1978)

Terror beyond imagination . . . Experience the most frightening moments of their lives . . . and yours

Beyond the Poseidon Adventure (1979)

The greatest adventure on *Earth!*

Capricorn One (1979)

**He is afraid.
He is totally alone . . .
He is 3 million light years from home . . .**

E.T. (1982)

Dirty Harry is at it again.

Sudden Impact (1984)

It all began with three faceless bodies in the snow . . .

Gorky Park (1984)

**First they betrayed him
Then they gambled with his life.**

The Honorary Consul (1984)

**He was Tony Montana
The world will remember him
By another name
Scarface
He loved the American Dream.
With a vengeance.**

Scarface (1984)

'The family that *slays* together, stays together.' Ma Barker

Bloody Mama (1970)

Comedies

Comedies come in all shapes and sizes. There's the silent variety that features stone-faced heroes, trembling heroines, beetle-browed villains, loveable tramps, human flies, cross-eyed comics, fat fools and funny policemen who keep falling off high-speed vehicles and bumping into each other. And there's the talking variety that offers absent-minded professors, dizzy blondes, mad mothers, idiot politicians, imbecile businessmen, lunatic lawyers, cretinous clergymen, chaps in drag, women in Army uniform, front pages and Philadelphia stories, seven year itches from blazing saddles, kind hearts and coronaries, graduates of great races, duck soup for doctors in the house, pink panthers with powerful producers, chumps at Oxford and nights at the opera, mad Wednesdays and miracles at Morgan's Creek, lives of Brian, Lavender Hill mobs, last remakes of Beau Geste, and everything you always wanted to know about sex but never had the strength to try. Comedy is a capacious metaphor.

The Silents thrived on stereotypes and many stars became clichés in themselves. When the Talkies came, verbal clichés joined forces with the visual. And a new breed established itself – actors and actresses who were in no way natural clown's like the Silent stars but who could handle comedy material superbly. Gag-writers grew in their thousands. The era of the wisecrack was upon us.

Trends have come and trends have gone but laughter is a constant. When all else fails, the comedy film can laugh at itself. Spoofs have become so standard that they aspire to stereotypical status. Modern talent does its best to breathe new life into old routines. Chases, funny fights, comical accidents, mistaken identity, marital mishaps, sporting fiascoes and hilarious journeys have stood the test of time. They – and other ingredients – are required seasoning.

It is a long road from Mack Sennett to Monty Python but that road keeps doubling back on itself. Comedy is the most durable of all the genres. Every film ever made comes within its provenance eventually. Anno domini makes clowns of us all.

Titles

Way Out West
Take the Money and Run
Never Give a Sucker an Even Break
Born Yesterday
Some Like it Hot
All Things Bright and Beautiful
Whose Been Sleeping in My Bed?
Bringing up Baby
You Can't Take it With You
Always Leave Them Laughing

Plots

Slapstick comedy about little man at odds with big world, and involving buckets of water, custard pies and extended chase sequences.

Screwball comedy in which the daily experience of living becomes a crazy adventure that borders on farce.

Black comedy which finds gallows humour in the darker aspects of the human condition such as crime, death or the payment of income tax.

Sexual comedy about men or women who can't get enough or who suffer from too much.

Satirical comedy which mercilessly mocks and deflates some element in society – with police and politicians as standard targets.

Sophisticated comedy about marriage or divorce in which both principals speak poniards and every word stabs.

Extravaganza that follows tortuous race between cars, boats, balloons, trains or magnificent men in their flying machines.

53

Musical comedy in which songs are used to get a laugh or heighten a romantic moment; and in which the clown always has the best numbers.

Spoof of another film genre, usually mixing satire with celebration.

Anarchic comedy in which conventional values and cherished institutions are subverted by zany characters who would be confined to mental homes in any other kind of film.

Characters

Tramps, outsiders, little chaps, Mr Averages and other Everyman figures who have comical struggles to survive in a hostile world.

The comic duo – two men, two women, one of each   whose routine is identical in each film even though storylines and settings may alter.

The comedy team made up of a number of clearly recognisable types, who carry on duplicating their performances in a variety of locations.

The innocent hero who suffers from an unfortunate resemblance to a master criminal, a politician or a king, and who is caught up in a comedy of mistaken identity.

The ordinary man, woman or married couple, who have fame, fortune or an unusual inheritance ('I bequeath my herd of buffalo and my haunted house . . .') thrust upon them in a way that transforms their life.

A minor character – court jester, barber, guard – who has a major effect on some crucial event in history.

The would-be adulterer caught with his trousers down by a vengeful, she-doesn't-understand-me wife.

The fool who holds down an important job – US President, Army general, French police inspector – that gives him endless scope for comically complicating the lives of all those around him.

Funny foreigners.

Comical kids and animals.

Dialogue

Here's another fine mess you've gotten me into.

Laurel and Hardy

Not that I care, but where is your husband?
   – Why, he's dead.
   –I'll bet he's just using that as an excuse.
   – I was with him till the end.
   – No wonder he passed away.
   – I held him in my arms and kissed him.
   – So it was murder!

Duck Soup

I started to walk down the street, when I heard a voice saying: 'Good evening, Mr Dowd.' I turned, and there was this great bit white rabbit leaning against a lamp-post. Well, I thought nothing of that! Because, when you've lived in a town as long as I've lived in this one, you get used to the fact that everybody knows your name . . .

Harvey

Why don't you slip out of those wet clothes and into a dry martini?

The Major and the Minor

This is the screwiest picture I was ever in.

Road to Morocco

Remember, men, we're fighting for this woman's honour . . . which is probably more than she ever did!

Duck Soup

Everybody wants to get into the act!

Jimmy Durante

My Great Aunt Jennifer ate a box of chocolates every day of her life. She lived to be a hundred and two, and when she had been dead three days she looked healthier than you do *now*.

The Man Who Came to Dinner

Marry me and I'll never look at another horse.

A Day at the Races

Tell me about my daddy. Is he really dead?
 – Well, we hope he is: they buried him.

Way Out West

They've broken the vestle with the pestle. The brew that is true
is in a flagon, with a picture of a dragon . . .

The Court Jester

If you ain't eating Wham,
You ain't eating ham!

Mr Blandings Builds His Dream House

Lemonade . . . in a dirty glass!

Road to Utopia

'Tain't a fit night out for a man nor beast!

The Fatal Glass of Beer

I'm a ba-a-a-a-ad boy!

Abbott and Costello

That's the dumbest thing I ever heard!

What's Up Doc?

Goodness what beautiful diamonds!
 – Goodness had nothing to do with it, dearie.

She Done Him Wrong

I am the Khasi.

Carry On Up the Khyber

Well, as Balzac used to say – there goes another novel!
Annie Hall

Typecasting

Carry On Playing It Again, Sam

Boris Goodenuff, a bad composer – **Danny Kaye**

Sir Cull, a Knight at the Opera – **The Marx Brothers**

Stage hands and piano shifters – **Laurel and Hardy**

A Chorus of Funny Foreigners – **Peter Sellers**

Rode-to-ruin, a palefaced horse – **Bob Hope**

Mezzo, a high soprano – **Dean Martin**

Follow-me, a juvenile lead – **George Burns**

Gillette, the Gay Blade – **Kenneth Williams**

Basso, a profundo with spectacles – **Woody Allen**

Cosy Fanny Tooty, an overture – **Mae West**

One In, One Out – an odd couple – **Jack Lemmon and Walter Matthau**

The Waltz Time Bandits – **Monty Python Team**

Barmaid, a counter tenor – **Barbra Streisand**

The History of Music, Part One – **Mel Brooks**

Annie, a Grand Finale – **Diane Keaton**

Everybody else in the film – **Alec Guinness**

Cops and Robbers

The motion picture industry has always invested heavily in crime. It has robbed banks and stolen art treasures and grabbed payrolls from security vans. It has run illegal gambling joints and sold bootleg liquor. It has subsidised the Mafia and dirtied its fingers with protection, prostitution and narcotics. Murder has been its top priority. Rape, arson, blackmail and fraud have been encouraged and juries have been bought by the dozen. Car thieves have prospered and violence has had a free hand.

Gangsters make good film stars. Their profession is a dramatic one and their private lives are fascinating. They may be tough guys who strut around in snap-brim hats and double-breasted jackets, or sophisticated family men kept together by a code of honour. They are the kings of organised crime and they rule with blood and iron.

The lone crook is a different species. He may be a small-time loser with a grudge against society or a justified sinner in revolt against tainted values. Whichever he is, you find him in the same bars and pool-halls and driving lots. He has a habit of stumbling into the big time and getting out of his depth. Mortuaries at the film studios are full of him.

Women get a raw deal out of crime. Gangsters and solo villains alike view the feminine gender through insensitive eyes. Molls and pick-ups and even wives must expect to be ignored, shouted at, groped, slapped around, betrayed, humiliated and even murdered. The lucky ones get away with a grapefruit in the kisser.

Whether it turns the spotlight on the cops or the robbers, whether it glorifies crime or villifies it, whether it ends with arrest or escape, the crime thriller reaches for the same stereotypes. Beatings, shootings, stabbings, stranglings, car chases, interrogations, court battles, prison break-outs, missing suspects, bribed witnesses, wry private investigators and renegade law-unto-themselves cops rule and roost. Justice is done and shown to be not done. And the film industry continues to float on the crime wave to the sandy beaches of profit and prestige.

Titles

Underworld
Scarface
The Public Enemy
Gun Crazy
Detective Story
G-Men
Kiss Me, Deadly
In Cold Blood
Bonnie and Clyde
Riot in Cell Block II

Plots

Godfatherdom.

Gang warfare during Prohibition.

Police corruption as a strong arm of crime.

Daring prison escape.

Hostage drama.

Police versus politicians in the big city.

Large-scale undercover operation to expose narcotics ring, numbers racket or vice empire.

Search for a missing person who is found dead and whose corpse is a signpost to a welter of intrigue and murder.

Progress of hoodlum from small time to big time.

Desperate race to get evidence to convict notorious criminal who is about to walk free.

Characters

Corpses galore.

Molls and worried mothers.

Al Capone, Baby Face Nelson, Dillinger and other real-life gangsters.

Philip Marlowe, Mike Hammer, Sam Spade and any other famous fictional detectives.

The tougher-than-the-tough-guys cop.

The decent men trapped into criminal activities.

Gum-chewing taxi-drivers, bartenders, janitors and doormen who have information at a price.

Single-minded cops who continue investigations in defiance of orders from above, get regular roastings from superiors, but solve the crime in the end.

Crooked mayors, judges, district attorneys and other authority figures.

Hoods, hit-men, bodyguards, frighteners, muscle.

Dialogue

You're going to treat yourself to a handful of clouds. I mean the kind that come out of the end of a .38 automatic.
   – I wouldn't mind the hot chair with you sitting on my lap.

Doorway to Hell

Look, Ma – top of the world!

White Heat

Your side of the fence is almost as dirty as mine.

– With one difference: we only hurt bad people.

Kiss of Death

No friends, no rest, no peace. Keep moving, that's all that's left for me.
 – Can't you tell me where you're going? Do you need money? How do you live?
 – I steal.

I Am a Fugitive From a Chain Gang

Listen, I've been rich and I've been poor. Believe me, rich is better.

The Big Heat

Hey, look at the monkeys! They think they're going to get Tony Camonte!

Scarface (1932)

I been taking orders from you for too long. You're through. Beat it – go, on scram! . . . Now if anyone turns yellow and squeals, my gun is going to speak its piece.

Little Caesar

Nothing wrong with shooting as long as the right people get shot.

Magnum Force

Little did I realise that what began in the back alleys of our little town would end in the badlands of Montana.

Badlands

I'm just a guy with a one-ton brain who's too nervous to steal and too lazy to work. I do other people's thinking for them and make them like it. I realise that all human beings have their weaknesses and all man-made laws in this country are made to protect honest people. And how many people will admit they're honest? Racketeering is just getting what the other guy's got in a nice way.

Quick Millions

If a guy hasn't got the strength to go straight, he turns yellow.

Beast of a City

Don Corleone: This war stops now.

The Godfather

Go ahead, punk. Make my day.

Sudden Impact.

This is a stick up!

Public Enemy

If you could use me again, call this number.
  – Day or night?
  – Night's better. I work during the day.

The Big Sleep

They're murderers. I know the law says they're not because I'm still alive, but that's not their fault.

Fury

Typecasting

The Big Heat, Sleep and Magnum of Little Caesar

Little Caesar, usurping hoodlum – **Edward G Robinson**

Big Caesar, posthumous Mafia king – **Marlon Brando**

Ex-priest turned cop – **Pat O'Brien**

Moll and murderess – **Faye Dunaway**

The hit-man and heavy – **Charlton Heston**

Mad stop-at-nothing cop – **Gene Hackman**

Gum-chewing taxi-driver – **Judd Hirsch**

The Body – **Raquel Welch**

Fantasy

Fantasy brings the best and the worst out of the film industry. It is a triumph of imagination and a treadmill of repetition, a world of wonder and a land of yawn, a thrilling voyage and a routine journey. One minute you believe a man can fly; the next, you believe the monsters are made out of pink string and sealing wax. Fantasy is a blend of extremes and this is what makes it so uniquely compelling. It's magic and mediocrity. Genius with a bad limp.

Ever since film-makers discovered the tricks of the camera they have astounded us with them. We've had mysterious disappearances, spectral apparitions, metamorphoses, mythical creatures, giants, dwarves, aliens, mutants, zombies, vampires, poltergeists, phantoms, devils, even conducted tours through the human body. Sometimes fantasy has leaned towards horror, sometimes towards science, and sometimes – like a bifocated Tower of Pisa – towards both at once. At all times, it has inclined towards entertainment.

Fantasy is a fun fair. Its noise and colour and flashing vitality are exhilarating. Its chairoplanes whirl us around in space, its dodgems give us bumps and thumps, and its ghost train offers us a cheap ride to terror. The scenic railway of its special effects will make us laugh and scream while its helter-skelter pace makes our head spin. On its carousel the horses gallop to the realms of the unknown; on its slot-machines the space invaders are for real.

Fifty years ago, *King Kong* beat his chest and said it all. The medium is the message. Love story, adventure thriller, monster movie, science fiction tale, comedy, tragedy, fairytale, parody – *Kong* was all this and more. It is the quintessential fantasy. Giant ape comes to the civilised world. For one magnificent night of destruction, he calls the shots. With a beautiful girl held firmly but gently in his hand, he climbs the

Empire State Building and battles it out with buzzing aeroplanes.

Using many clichés and creating many more, *King Kong* showed the way. Thanks to him and others, fantasy has become the Eighth Wonder of the World – coming to your local cinemas very soon!

Titles

Superman
King Kong
Star Wars
Alien
Battlestar Galactica
Metropolis
Freaks
Planet of the Apes
Batman
The Lost World

Plots

Mankind saved by being with superhuman powers.

Remote island with weird monsters.

Inter-galactic warfare.

Invasions from Outer Space.

Animals rule over humans.

Discovery of strange lost world in uncharted territory or beneath the sea.

Bleak view of the effect of automation on the future of Earth.

Diabolism in the ordinary family.

Post-holocaust survivors turn to savagery.

Mankind terrorised by beings who return from the dead, emerge from the sea, grow in the garden or appear from the most unexpected sources.

Characters

Supermen and superwomen.

Mad explorers who track down prehistoric monsters.

Sadistic rulers of empires in space.

Children possessed by the Devil.

Monsters who disobey their creators and go off on a murderous rampage.

Birds, apes and any other domestic or wild animals that turn on mankind with a vengeance.

Time-travellers.

Vampires, zombies, ghosts, ghouls, poltergeists and other threats to a good night's sleep.

The loveable alien who falls to Earth by mistake and who enlarges the perceptions of mankind.

Latter-day Faust figures who sell their soul to the Devil in return for earthly riches and power.

Dialogue

May the Force be with you!

Star Wars

Kill, then, love . . . When you have known that, you have known everything . . .

The Most Dangerous Game

Get away from that lever – you'll blow us all to atoms!

The Old Dark House

Something monstrous, all-powerful, still living, still holding that island in hideous fear.

King Kong

Listen to them . . . creatures of the night. What music they make!

Dracula

Synthetic flesh! Synthetic flesh!

Doctor X

All the universe or nothing: which shall it be?

Things to Come

We'll start with a few murders. Big men. Little men. Just to show we make no distinctions.

The Invisible Man

A soul? A soul is nothing. Can you see it? Smell it? Touch it? No . . .

All That Money Can Buy

Me, Tarzan. You, Jane.

Tarzan, the Ape Man

At the moment the creature is keeping him alive. If we remove it, we risk losing Kane.
   – We have to take that chance.
   – What do you propose to do? It won't pull off.
   – We'll have to try cutting it off. The sooner we remove it, the better it's likely to be for Kane.
   – I don't like it but I see your point.

Alien

I know you have a civil tongue in your head – I sewed it there myself.

Teenage Frankenstein

He was the best star pilot in the galaxy and a cunning warrior.

Star Wars

She was very beautiful when she died . . . a hundred years ago.

Dracula's Daughter

It was beauty killed the beast.

King Kong

Look, he communicates through you. He belongs to you. But you gotta make it legal. My dad's a lawyer. He'll figure something out. We'll be millionaires, we'll go everywhere. Everyone will want to know us because we'll be the most famous boys in the world. They'll all want to meet E.T. And he'll be *ours*.

E.T.

How could I have been so completely wrong? I have led the entire human race to ruin!

Battlestar Galactica

Typecasting

Alien Bride of Jedi Ape from Mars meets Son of Abbott and Costello at Phantom Opera II about Clockwork Orange of Dr Caligari.

Darth Vampire, a high Blood Count – **Christopher Lee**

The 2001st Space Odysseus – **Harrison Ford**

Mad Scientist of Lost World – **Peter Cushing**

Sarsparilla, a fizzer from space – **Jane Fonda**

Miss Tickle-my-tummy, a victim – **Fay Wray**

King Kong's hunchbacked Mummy – **Boris Karloff**

Flasher Gordon, an exhibitionist – **Dick Van Dyke**

Faust, the Wolf Man of Virginia – **Richard Burton**

The Man Who Fell To Earth Drunk – **Wilfred Lawson**

The Tory Wet from Outer Space – **Claude Rains**

Historical Hokum

History is the Costume Hire Department of the film industry. Dressed in style, even the worst screenplay can have a certain dash and elegance; by the same token, however, even the best story can be obscured if the most eye-catching performances come from the cozzies. *The Private Life of Queen Elizabeth* starring a dress in the Spanish fashion with stiff lace collar and satin sleeves decorated with ribbons, pearls and gems of assorted colours!

Because action is a vital ingredient, it is essential to retain the services of the finest fight arranger in Hollywood. The cleverest choreographer will be needed to teach the actors to move and dance in their unaccustomed garb, and the most musical composer will be brought in to bathe the whole thing in a pastiche of period sound. One thing about historical pictures – they give the guys on sackbut, lute and medieval harp a chance to earn a penny!

Language, of course, is critical and it is essential to employ writers who have mastered the esperanto of the costume epic. It is no good slinging in the odd 'My lord, the carriage waits' or 'I' faith, the master hath a ready wit!'. The screenplay must be written in high seriousness and contain hundreds of standard phrases, idioms and unusual word-orders. Only if the language has a true cod-historical ring to it can the actors stand a chance against the costumes. A line like 'I haven't lived like a King; perhaps I can die like one' will see off any regalia. And a put-down like 'I advise you to curb that wagging tongue, you insolent rascal' will be the match for any medieval attire.

Finally, of course, there is the high adventure that a film has the right to expect if it goes back in time. Excitement, intrigue, murder, romance, treason, assassination and chases on horseback come thick and fast, and those costumes mean that someone will always appear in disguise at some point. What's past is past, and what we see of it on the screen is pure entertainment. It is watching the French Revolution without being in any danger of a shave from the national razor.

Titles

Robin Hood
Captain Blood
The Prisoner of Zenda
The Three Musketeers
Mutiny on the Bounty
The Count of Monte Cristo
Ivanhoe
The Scarlet Pimpernel
The Thief of Baghdad
The Buccaneer

Plots

Oppressive régimes forcing good men into outlawry where they merrily rob the rich to feed the poor.

Bloodthirsty pirates ruling waves until gallant hero infiltrates and betrays them to their doom.

High adventure in Ruritania.

Swordplay and intrigue in the Musketeers.

Mutiny aboard a ship of the King's navy.

Elaborate vengeance wreaked by escaped prisoner on those who had him unjustly incarcerated.

Knightly exploits in medieval England.

Daring rescue of French aristocrats from Madame Guillotine in Revolutionary Times.

Rags to riches story of urchin from Middle East.

American president forced to rely on notorious pirate while repelling British attack in 1812.

Characters

Outlaws who do good.

Villainous relatives who usurp thrones.

Comical friars, servants, seamen, shopkeepers and kids.

Apparently vain and feckless men who lead a double-life as heroic adventurers.

Breathless and beautiful heroines who are glad of a man's superior strength in a man's world.

Foolish kings, innkeepers and palace guards.

Wise and loyal wrinkly retainers.

Evil sorcerers whose magic powers are somehow thwarted by the forces of Good.

Chivalrous knights who risk their lives for the sake of a lady's honour.

Tyrannical sea-captains.

Dialogue

This Tartar woman is for me – and my blood says 'take her'.

The Conqueror

I'll brook no mutiny, Mr Christian, sir!

Mutiny on the Bounty (1935)

Five years spent on a tunnel that leads not to freedom – but to another man's cell!

The Count of Monte Cristo

After all, tomorrow is another day . . .

Gone With the Wind

Aw, truly this is the Son of God.

The Greatest Story Ever Told

Nothing like this has come to Rome since Romulus and Remus!

Cleopatra

I don't need that spear. It's only a young lion.

Samson and Delilah

He's the deadliest archer in England.

The Adventures of Robin Hood (1938)

Be faithful and His Majesty will reward you beyond your dreams . . .

The Prisoner of Zenda (1937)

Odds fish, Sir Percy, you're brainless, spineless and useless, but you do know clothes.

The Scarlet Pimpernel (1934)

Gather round, lads and lasses!

The Crimson Pirate

But he's *not* dead! That's the point. At least, not really dead.
   – Galen, I saw him die. Tyrian stabbed him. He's dead. He's burnt.
   – Yes, but he's a sorcerer, don't you see? That's what we've forgotten all this time. It's a matter of faith. Of seeing.
   – I know what *I* saw – a sword going in one side of a man and out the other. Are you going to tell me that that man is alive?

Dragonslayer

By all that I have done for France – by all that I have written, I swear to you that Dreyfus is innocent. May all that melt away – may my name be forgotten if Dreyfus is not innocent. He *is* innocent.

The Life of Emile Zola

These are modern times . . . 1804.

Forever and a Day

Yer beautiful in yer wrath.

The Conqueror

If you can't trust the biggest banker in France, who can you trust?

The Count of Monte Cristo

You're a man after my own heart, Rassendyll. Frankly, we're the only two worth saving out of this entire affair . . . What did they teach you on the playing fields of England?
 – Chiefly, not to throw knives at other people's backs. Bad-tempered fellow, aren't you, under all that charm?

The Prisoner of Zenda (1937)

In all the forest there isn't a hunter as good as me.

The Adventures of Robin Hood (1938)

Typecasting

The Crimson Son of the Mark of Zorro

Finest Swordsman in all Films – **Douglas Fairbanks**

Wicked King or Captain – **Charles Laughton**

Jolly Good Fellow – **Alan Hale**

Proud Wrinkly Retainer – **C Aubrey Smith**

Lady at Pirates' Mercy – **Maureen O'Hara**

Comical Irish Revolutionary – **Noel Purcell**

Bold outlaw, pirate or soldier – **Errol Flynn**

Literature

Film-makers have always raided literature with Viking enthusiasm. They have plundered its treasures, burned its homesteads, and carried off its womenfolk. Once pillaged, a classic is still not assured of safety. The Vikings may return at any moment in their long cheque-boats to re-plunder, re-burn, re-carry off and of course, to re-cast.

The Great Books of the World have a lot going for them. They are known, loved and cherished. They have good stories. They lend status, significance and respectability. Most important of all, their authors are frequently dead and out of copyright. There is no better co-writer than a Russian genius who died in 1881. It is the perfect act of collaboration: Dostoevsky provides the story and the saleable title, and the Fifth Rewrite Man does the rest. Dead men alter no tales.

Because the classics are known rather than read, it is possible to take the most enormous liberties without being found out. Indeed, this is part of the fun of it. The cliché classic, for instance, would be *Wuthering Heights* with half the story left out; or *Anna Karenina* giving the impression that Levin is a minor character; or *Jane Eyre* in which Mr Rochester is played by a hell-raising American general. Language and geographical barriers do not exist. A French Count may speak with a Texan drawl and a Welsh village may pop up in the San Fernando Valley. Film is another country: they do things differently there.

Astonishingly enough, the results are nearly always worthwhile. Literary masterpieces can survive anything and come up smiling. They are screened with such disarming simplicity and attended by such irresistible cliché casting that it is churlish to complain. Classic fiction has consistently produced classic film. Those who bleat about rape and pillage should remember it could be worse.

Next time the Vikings come they may want to change a title and musicalise.

Titles

Rebecca
Anna Karenina
Tess
Jane Eyre
Women in Love
The Grapes of Wrath
Tom Jones
Moby Dick
How Green was My Valley
Wuthering Heights

Plots

Woman marries English nobleman and lives in the shadow of his former wife.

Eternal triangle in nineteenth-century Russia.

Rural saga of exploited peasant girl driven to murder.

Romance between orphan girl and wealthy but mysterious gentleman.

Love strives to overcome class and other barriers.

Social realism.

Rude, raucous, rumbustious, period romp.

Man versus symbolic white whale.

Evocation of life in the Welsh valleys.

Tormented love affair in wind-swept Yorkshire.

Characters

Outsiders who meet resistance getting in.

Unfaithful wives tortured by guilt.

Girls who are victims of their own beauty.

Mysterious gents with secret sorrows.

Free-thinking women who defy convention.

The common people.

Lascivious ladies and drunken squires.

Strange men driven by a single obsession.

Welsh common people.

Primitives.

Dialogue

You thought I loved Rebecca? You thought I killed her, loving her? She was incapable of love, of tenderness, of decency.

Rebecca

Keep still, you young devil, or I'll cut your throat!

Great Expectations

At this moment it is difficult to believe that you are so proud.
   – At this moment it is difficult to believe that you are so prejudiced.

Pride and Prejudice

Yes, I killed him. And I'm glad, I tell you. Glad, glad, glad!

The Letter

Clear out, Hannay, they'll get you next!

The Thirty-Nine Steps

Rich fellas come up, an' they die, an' their kids ain't no good, an' they die out. But we keep a-comin'. We're the people that live. Can't nobody wipe us out. Can't nobody lick us. We'll go on forever, Pa. We're the people.

The Grapes of Wrath

Call me Ishmael . . .

Moby Dick

Tell her – Barkis is willin'.

David Copperfield

Oh my heart's darling! Hear me this time, at last! Cathy, I love you! Come in to me: come to me, Cathy, my own . . .

Wuthering Heights (1939)

Where the devil are my slippers, Eliza?

Pygmalion

All animals are equal but some animals are more equal than others.

Animal Farm

And at home by the fire, whenever you look up, there I shall be – and whenever I look up, there will be you.

Far From the Madding Crowd

He's gone after the treasure. Without me. Me, who lay dreaming of treasure.

King Solomon's Mines

Gimme visky . . . ginger ale on the side. And don't be stingy, baby.

Anna Christie

Love is the morning and the evening star . . .

Elmer Gantry

It is a far, far better thing that I do now than I have ever done . . .

A Tale of Two Cities

Big Brother is watching you.

1984

Five thousand pounds a year and unmarried! That's the best piece of news since Waterloo!

Pride and Prejudice

Oh, if you had seen it, Countess! And his wife was there . . . it was awful to see her! . . . She flung herself on the body. They say he was the only support of an immense family. How awful!

Anna Karenina

I love to feel your arm *there*. It rests me so.

Sons and Lovers

Typecasting

Far from the Madding Classics

Anna Christie, an open invitation – **Greta Garbo**

Gabriel Oak, her faithful lover – **Alan Bates**

Moby Dick, the Go-Between – **Warren Beatty**

Mr Polly, the historian – **John Mills**

Vronsky, a Smirnov drinker – **Robert Newton**

Lady Chatterley, the gamekeeper's woman – **Meryl Streep**

Big Brother – **Sylvester Stallone**

Mr Rochester, a strange gentleman – **W C Fields**

Mrs Danvers, a sinister housekeeper – **Danny la Rue**

Mr Darcy, a proud man at a ball – **John Travolta**

She – **Jane Fonda**

It – **Lon Chaney Jr**

Spies

All films are spy films. Unseen in the dark, we keep them under surveillance and preserve salient details on the microfilm of our memories. The intelligence is then passed on to colleagues who decide whether or not to act on it. As in real-life espionage, much of our work is dull, prosaic and repetitive but there is always the chance of the valuable document that makes all the waiting worthwhile.

Spies have been cliché characters in films since the beginning. History has helped the genre along. When America entered the Great War in 1917, the spy film had a tremendous boost. It seemed that no movie was complete without its quota of sinister German agents plotting fiendish plots on behalf of the Fatherland. During the 1920's spy fever swept across Europe and it found its expression in hissing Silents like Fritz Lang's *Spies*. Here the protagonist is Haghi, super-spy, master of disguise, brilliant intellect, and head of a dedicated army of male and female agents. Haghi filled the screen as completely as King Kong and he was introduced by the inter-title card: **Who is at the bottom of all this?** This is at once a question and a definition of the whole genre.

Since the Second World War added its impetus, there has been no holding the spy film. It has inhabited every corner of the globe and explored every device in the codebook. The adventure of spying has been a continuous theme with the trade glamourised and glorified by James Bondery. Romance has been another key element with a spy being frequently called upon to betray the woman or man that he or she loves.

Psychological thrillers became voguish and spies were subjected to brain-washing, mind-bending and drug-induced hypnosis. Political chicanery is always there somewhere and many films sought to expose the governmental machinations that make espionage necessary. Wartime spies, of course, are another story – and it has been told many times. Humour has not been exiled and the wry, amusing spy is another cliché. One thing is certain: the film of betrayal never lets us down.

Titles

Spies
Cloak and Dagger
State Secret
Double Agent
The Counterfeit Traitor
Codeword
Pimpernel Smith
Undercover
Special Assignment
High Treason
Confessions of a Nazi Spy

Plots

Find the Mole.

Rescue of VIP from war-torn country.

Exchange of captured spies.

Love story between spies on opposing sides.

Brain-washing techniques used to create a trained assassin who can be planted back in his own country and triggered at the crucial moment.

Mission impossible ('There's only one man who can handle this assignment') against crazed master-criminal.

Routine assignment that turns out to have unseen dangers and problems.

Sabotage and subterfuge used to create wars in troublesome countries.

VIP flees country and seeks asylum elsewhere in order to find out state secrets in his new homeland.

Capture and interrogation of enemy agents.

Characters

The super-spy in the James Bond mould.

The lovely but unscrupulous female spy.

The embittered agent who becomes disillusioned with espionage but is not allowed to resign.

The urbane, cards-close-to-the-chest head of British intelligence.

The innocent man or woman caught up in spying and having to fight for survival.

Chase-me-Charlie spies whose cover is blown and who spend the entire film on the run.

The contact who, when the hero reaches him, is already dead.

The girl used to bait the spy-trap.

The master of disguise.

The distraught wife who learns that her loving husband, by day a Professor of Mathematics, is by night ('And you always told me you were working late in your study') a daring spy.

Dialogue

Café Mozart, eight o'clock . . .

The Third Man

Oh, Victor, please don't go to the underground meeting tonight.

Casablanca

We have ways of making men talk.

Lives of a Bengal Lancer

We've been engaged in some rather tough work here. I think we're coping moderately well with the situation in other parts of the country, but it's getting a little out of hand in Berlin. They're quite a tough bunch. Nazi from top to toe. In the classic tradition. But not just the remains of the old lot. There's quite a bit of new blood. Youth. Firm believers. Very dangerous. It won't do to underestimate them.

The Quiller Memorandum

But the suicide letter –
 – I wrote it. Freitag brought the paper and I wrote it. The signature was already there. Samuel's signature . . . Take your hands off me! Do you think I'm yours because I don't belong to them? Go away! Go away and kill Freitag and Dieter, keep the game alive, Mr Smiley. But don't think I'm on your *side*, do you hear?

The Deadly Affair

My friend, you have heard the whole story and now you have seen the evidence. Will you help me? Will you help me save this girl? It is my only chance that you will give her hope. That you will give her a reason to live. Will you?
 – I do not see that I can help. What is it you have in mind?
 – I wish you to pay court to my daughter and marry her. On the day of the marriage, I will give you a personal dowry of one million pounds in gold . . .

On Her Majesty's Secret Service

I never knew the old Vienna before the war, with its Strauss music, its glamour and easy charm. I really got to know it in the classic period of the black market – we'd run anything if people wanted it enough and had the power to pay . . .

The Third Man

Dry martini. Shaken, not stirred.

Doctor No

As leader of all illegal activities in Casablanca, I'm a very influential and respected man.

Casablanca

And then what?
  – Kill him.
  – Kill him!
  – You know the score . . .

Telefon

Who was our leading operator here in the last file you saw?
  – Metzler.
  – He's dead. Another colleague of yours took over from him. Kenneth Lindsay Jones.
  – Uh-huh.
  – He's dead, too. He was killed two days ago. Long range nine point three, in the spine . . . We'd like you to take over.

The Quiller Memorandum

Typecasting

The Deadly Affair of the Quiller Memorandum to the Manchurian Candidate Left Out in the Cold with Scorpio, Dr No, and the Mata Hari who went North by Northwest on the Night Train to Munich.

Deadpan restaurateur spy – **Humphrey Bogart**

Head of British Intelligence – **Harry Andrews**

CIA agent as top physicist – **Paul Newman**

Wily KGB Colonel – **Oscar Homolka**

The beautiful counter-spy – **Marlene Dietrich**

The MacGuffin – **Alfred Hitchcock**

Westerns

The Western is a horse. It is fed on clichés, shod with stereotypes, and whipped into a gallop by the latest trend. They change its name, its breed, its colour, its saddle and its rider, but its neigh is unmistakable. It pulls stagecoaches, hearses, covered wagons and runaway buckboards. It carries cowboys, Indians, sheriffs, outlaws and rescuing cavalry. The sound of a gun is music to its ear. War, fear, love, lust, ambition, vengeance and violence are its stable companions. Death is its blacksmith. It is mythical and real, animal and human, a beast of burden and a wonderful one-two-three-four-legged friend. It is good, bad and ugly.

Action was the keynote of *The Great Train Robbery* (1903) and its example guided the Silents. The robbery on a moving train, the dividing of spoils at the outlaw hideout and the final gun battle with the posse became stock scenes. Other clichés followed. The pianist at the picture house was kept busy. Until the Talkies . . .

A powerful story of 9 strange people

Stagecoach (1939) is the Model-T Ford of the talking Western. Drunken doctor, gentleman gambler, soft-hearted whore, crooked banker, meek whisky-drummer, pregnant wife, cheery driver, conscientious sheriff and wanted man share a journey that changes their lives. These nine strange people have been well-known types ever since.

> Arizona. Indians thronging.
> Arrows pinging. Pistols ponging.
> Something smelly – old and hoary.
> Not to worry: it's the story.

In trying to avoid one set of clichés, directors have created others. We have had the epic Western, the vendetta Western, the romantic Western, the horror Western, the comedy Western, the send-up Western, the Peckinpah authentic Western, and the Western as a vehicle for myths from other countries. But the old horse never lets us down. No matter what goes in one end, it comes out much the same at the other. It's priceless entertainment and good for the garden.

Titles

Stagecoach
The Iron Horse
Stampede
The Gunfighter
Wagonmaster
Billy the Kid
High Noon
Rio Bravo
Lawman
Apache

Plots

Wild frontier town tamed by new sheriff.

Wagon train heads west to misadventure.

Indians on warpath against beleaguered fort.

Cattle drive hit by weather, stampede and rustlers.

Desperate struggle between Union Pacific and Central Pacific to build first transcontinental railway.

Small community hires gunmen to protect it.

Pony Express or Wells Fargo.

Outlaws return to take revenge on the sheriff who sent them to prison, and who gets no backing from the terrified townspeople.

The chase film. Baddies tracked through burning desert and snow-capped mountains until they are finally brought to book.

The spoof western.

Characters

The crooked saloon owner who runs the whole town.

The tough lawman who defeats a whole gang on his own.

The whore with the heart of gold.

The drunkard who doubles as town philosopher.

The good Indian who argues for peace but whose words are ignored by his warlike colleagues.

Comical deputies.

Hard-boiled wagonmasters who get the train through.

The loner who drifts into town, solves its problems, has a brief but poignant love affair with the heroine, then rides out into the sunset.

Retired gunfighters who are forced into one last shoot-out to vindicate their reputation.

Billy the Kid, Jesse James, Wyatt Earp, Geronimo, Big Chief Sitting Bull, General Custer, Butch Cassidy, the Sundance Kid and other legendary figures who are used either to enforce a myth or explode it.

Dialogue

Least I'll be remembered . . .
Pat Garrett and Billy the Kid

Until the Apache are taken or destroyed . . .
Major Dundee

You lookin' for trouble, Donovan?
  – You aimin' to help me find it, Liberty?

The Man Who Shot Liberty Valance

You see, in the world there are two types of people, my friend. Those with loaded guns and those who dig. You dig.

The Good, the Bad and the Ugly

When you side with a man you stick with him. If you can't do that you're worse than some animal.

The Wild Bunch

When you say that, smile.

The Virginian

Come and see a fat old man some time.

True Grit

Deep among the lonely sunbaked hills of Texas, the great and weatherbeaten stone still stands . . .

Duel in the Sun

I can't swim.
  – Don't worry. The fall will probably kill you.

Butch Cassidy and the Sundance Kid

Well, I still gotta ranch across the border. A real nice place. Trees, grass, water . . . There's a cabin half-built. A man could live there. With a woman . . . Would you go?

Stagecoach

My father says there's right and wrong, good and evil. It isn't that simple, is it?
  – No. It should be but it isn't.

Ride the High Country

90

All gunfighters are lonely. They live alone and die without a dime, a woman or a friend.

Gunfight at the O.K. Corral

Iron men and iron horses – that's progress.

Dodge City

Cheyenne's right. Once you killed four, it's easy to make it five.

Once Upon a Time in the West

How did he do it, Pa? I only hear one shot.
 – It's a question of speed, son.
 – Pa – ain't nobody faster on the draw than him?
 – Faster than him? Nobody.

My Name is Nobody

Ringo asked me to marry him. Is that wrong for a girl like me? If a man and woman love each other?
 – You're going to be hurt, child, worse than you've ever been hurt before. Don't you know that boy's headed for prison?

Stagecoach

Typecasting

The Magnificent Wild Bunch from the Big Country who shot Liberty Valance and Shane in a Duel in the Sun near Red River for a Fistful of Dollars.

Gritty, one-eyed shootist – **John Wayne**

Walk-tall, taciturn loner – **Clint Eastwood**

Pistol-packin' momma – **Shelley Winters**

Real mean hombre – **Lee van Cleef**

His comical sidekick – **Jack Elam**

Belle, the saloon girl – **Mae West**

Decent man forced to kill – **James Stewart**

Tobaccy-chewin' deputy – **Walter Brennan**

Newspapers

The origin of the newspaper is lost in the mists of *The Times*. It is the elder statesman in a juvenile Commons, the calm voice of reason in a screaming world, a horn of plenty with supplementary benefits. The 199-year-old Pharoah of the Fourth Estate set standards of presentation, impartiality and moral probity which – thank goodness – other newspapers have done their level best to ignore. They are in a different ball game. *The Times* purveys a Mandarin style: its competitors sell mandarin oranges. You pays your money and you takes your choice. Journalism or Juice.

Though the Grand Old Man has developed a whole range of distinctive habits, poses and nervous tics, our concern here is with his illegitimate children. We listen to their howling headlines, their congenital puns, their eternal cries of 'Wolf!', their bawling bad jokes, their compulsive name-dropping and their ceaseless small-talk about the weather. In short, we luxuriate in all the things that makes the free press the richest repository of clichés that we possess. It loads every rift with ore. The watchdog of democracy wears a collar of pure gold and a silver disc that tells its age.

O Henry said it all. In his classic short story, *Calloway's Code*, a New York paper sends its special correspondent to the Russo-Japanese-Portsmouth War. Because all information is censored before it leaves the front, the wily Calloway devises an ingenious code and sends this cablegram.

'Foregone preconcerted rash witching goes muffled rumour mine dark silent unfortunate richmond existing great hotly brute select mooted parlous beggars ye angel incontrovertible.'

Thinking it harmless the authorities let it through. Back in America his colleagues realise that he has written in 'newspaper English' and that they simply have to complete the cliché to decipher the code.

'Conclusion arrangement act hour of midnight without saying report hath it host horse majority pedestrians (infantry) in the field conditions White Way contested force few question times description correspondent unawares fact.'

For his consummate skill in pulling the wool over the eyes of the Russian Bear, Calloway was rewarded with a promotion. He is now the editor on every tabloid newspaper in the known world. His code is nothing less than the small coin that jingles in the pocket of journalism. He has not forgotten his old colleagues on the New York *Enterprise*. One of them has become his right-hand man. Ames. Let us recall how O Henry describes this paragon of press virtue.

'Ames was the king-pin, the snowy-petalled marguerite, the star-bright looloo of the rewrite men. He saw attempted murder in the pains of green-apple colic, cyclones in the summer zephyr, lost children in every top-spinning urchin, an uprising of the down-trodden masses in every hurling of a derelict potato at a passing automobile.'

Yes, Ames is still around in a big way. He walks tall on the street of shame and can squeeze through the letterbox of every household in the land. He is It. The unbroken mould of newspaper know-how.

The Ames of Journalism may be summarised thus:

Immediacy – Ugly face of Britain today.
Dramatisation – Death riddle of mercy dash budgie.
Personalisation – I witness end of world!
Simplification – Pills cure earthquake.
Titillation – Cardinal, 70, jilted by nun, 15, in lesbian orgy.
Humour – Dog warden's stray success in Barking.
Novelty – Man bites stuffed mongoose in vice probe.

True professionals will also have a mastery of alliteration and assonance. It is a sure-fire way to grab a reader with a headline. Ames himself could not have bettered this example from the *News of the World* (July, 1983)

Dallas dolls dress to kill the dishes of Dynasty.

What immortal hand or eye framed this fearful symmetry? It is immediate, dramatic, personal, simple, titillating, humorous and as new as old hat. It is joy unconfined and service with a smile. It is the star to every wandering newshound and will save him from baying at the moon.

O little town of Amesville!

The cliché has come home again. Its birth was an honourable event in the dignified history of printing. It was conceived in the heat of typographical reproduction and it follows in its father's footsteps. Open any newspaper and see for yourself. The cliché has come home to roost!

Editorials

Porridge with jam on it
Just like Butlin's – the public view of what life is like in prison is not far off the mark, despite every effort to persuade us that we have it all wrong. Read the astonishing evidence on Page 3 today from Springhill Open Prison where sex, drugs and booze seem more freely available than in Soho.

Labour's dream ticket to a new tomorrow
Opportunity knocks for the Labour Party and Neil Kinnock. What a marvellous chance they have this week to lick themselves into shape; to **SHOW** us they are a radical party of vision and compassion; to **RAISE** their heads from petty internal squabbles and **LIFT** the people's aspirations.

Breeding a reign of fear
The fear that something in the air – nameless, unfelt and invisible – might slowly kill us all was once a basic plot of science fiction. Today, for some people, it is a fact of life.

The Yorkshire TV allegations about cases of cancer near

the nuclear plant at Windscale were chilling even to those living hundreds of miles from Cumbria.

Salute to brave Lech

In all the history of the Nobel Peace Prize there has never been a more worthy winner than Lech Walesa. Just four years ago the world had not even heard of the little man with the heavy moustache . . . He was just one among countless toiling millions denied basic rights and human dignity by the Communist dictators.

Dead, but not yet buried

Will the trade unions ever learn the simple truth that stopping work every time there is an argument over pay is a relic of a bygone age? With three million plus unemployed and a great fight going on for economic recovery, it is obscene for those in work to down tools when they want a few extra feathers in their nest.

Greed

Well, well, would you believe it? A rebellion at last in the Tory ranks. What were these revolting Tory MP's so steamed up about? The plight of the unemployed? The Chancellor cheating the pensioners? The outrageous profits of British Telecom? The desperate state of some of our hospitals? No fear. Their passions were aroused over the sacred question of their pay.

High-speed rip-off

Gas users should burn with high-speed fury over the latest attempts to put up the prices. They are the victims of a gigantic rip-off that makes the Great Train robbery look like petty pilfering.

The final sting? Muhammed Ali returns to Britain

Gone are the jibes that were once as smart as the jabs. Gone are the poems that were part of the fleet-footed choreography that turned a cocky Cassius Clay into the boxing idol of the world.

The words come more slowly. The spring has left his dancing feet. For years he showed 'em how to sting like a bee, but how sad now to see that this once-great athlete has paid boxing's cruel price for all those batterings in the ring.

Features

Is this the end of the corridor for the tea lady?

The rumours that sweep the corridors of power are just too far-fetched. Everyone is being fired? Mrs Thatcher's Daimler has been spotted in the car park? A *tea machine* is being installed? Oh, come on!

I happen to be able to settle any uncertainties arising and I happily do so. All these rumours are true and my advice to civil servants is to hide the teapot *now*.

Having a giggle with Sir Dancealot

John Travolta is The Body. Stripped for action in his new film, *Staying Alive*, his new shape is nothing short of sexsational. Fine muscles gleaming with energy, a perfect sculpted form, he is powerful without being Popeye. You too could have a body like this if you trained as Travolta did . . .

Inside the love nest of a kept woman

She lives in luxury but must always keep in the shadows. She appears to have everything but her very existence is a lie. *She* is The Kept Woman – that special breed in whose arms rich and successful husbands can find comforts their wives cannot provide.

Naff off, Anne: your verdict on Her Royal Haughtiness

The message from the nation to Princess Anne this morning is brutally frank. Most folk have had about enough of her royal haughtiness and bouts of bad temper . . .

The brides really waiting for Randy Andy

While Prince Andrew romps in the surf with a succession of sun-bronzed beauties, back home the serious business of choosing a suitable bride for him is under way. Home Counties mothers with long titles and fat incomes are grooming their daughters for a Royal game, set and match with the Romeo Prince.

My daughter is a gay

Secretary Jackie Charlton invited her mum to dinner at her flat to break the news that she was gay. It was a cosy scene. Just the two of them and a pile of pork chops and vegetables . . .

Great perfume test shock

Today we take the top off the great perfume myth. As the whiff of scandal over the fake Chanel No. 5 hangs in the air we reveal what no woman wants to admit . . . Sorry, ladies, but it seems you *can't* always believe your noses.

Love tricks won me my man, says Toyah

One long, lingering look was all it took for stormy singer Toyah to realise that she was hopelessly, head-over-heels in love with Tom Taylor.

Sexy Selleck

He is television's Number One male sex symbol. In a magazine poll women voted him that most wanted, needed, sexiest, most handsome man on telly. The name: Tom Selleck, star of the detective series, *Magnum P1*. Three years ago Tom, now 38, was unknown. But *Magnum* has turned him into the hottest, hunkiest TV actor around.

The Front Page

Headlines

Phew! It's a scorcher!

Terror ride of Top TV stars.

Superdad sponger's lover no. 3.

Drunken rampage of twenty cops.

Head jilts lover to wed daughter, 16.

Gun-run girl slips the net.

Chained: handcuffed De Lorean faces court.

Branded a killer: torment of love-nest murder husband.

The sauna tomb of a model: rich wife's head is found.

7 brides for Mr Bigamy: fiery Fred just loved weddings.

From Russia with love: British girl lures KGB man to West.

I was to die at 5 pm – doctor tells of 'hit' plot.

Cash row superstar says 'I'll sort it out'.

Murdered beach girl betrayed her lover.

Drama of swoop after break-in at top men's store.

Stories

Shamed Tory Minister Cecil Parkinson last night was ready to ride out the storm over his love child – thanks to the unshakable loyalty of Mrs Thatcher.

Today the *Daily Star* can reveal the heartbreaking truth about the man who is a legend.
   Muhammed Ali, arguably the greatest boxer who ever lived, is today a rambling figure who inhabits the wreckage of a once-magnificent body.

You're fired! That is the shock news for Coronation Street superstar Peter Adamson.

Tormented doctor Robert Jones talked yesterday of his fear of another knock on the door by detectives hunting his wife's brutal killer.
   'The finger of suspicion is being pointed at me,' he said.

Ambush victim Steven Waldorf last night lashed at the two policemen who shot him: 'They didn't even say sorry.'

And as the crack-down continues this weekend, they have already seized a mountain of filth.

A screaming, knife-wielding mob brought terror to a seaside town yesterday.
   Four people were rushed to hospital with serious wounds as

the gang rampaged along the seafront, punching and stabbing anyone in their way.

Britain's first heart 'op' on a dog looked to be a tail-wagging success last night.

The mother of a sex beast who killed a woman while on bail told last night of her horror at the court's decision to free him.

Gossip and showtalk

It's a hard night's day!
Rocking the night away at a London party is top TV inquisitor, Sir Robin Day. Hard to believe that the bow-tied scourge of evasive politicians will be 60 this month. Lady Day diplomatically describes her husband's dancing as 'passable'.

Broken-Hart! Wagner in love bust-up
That cry-on-the-shoulder romance between Hollywood stars Robert Wagner and Jill St John is over. Hart to Hart-throb Wagner found solace . . .

Teeing up trouble
Golf star Tony Jacklin is being threatened with the ultimate punishment for deciding to go into Spanish tax exile. His portrait may be removed from Scunthorpe Town Hall.

Linda leads the field!
Luscious horse-lover Linda Lusardi reins supreme in the beauty stakes – she always sends punters' pulses racing. Linda is betting on the 3-1 favourite, Ribot, to win the big Sun-William Hill race of champions. Of course some gamblers might put their shirts on another nag . . . in which case, turf luck!

The man-eater tamed by love
The bitch of Crossroads, man-eater Miranda Pollard, has been tamed – by the man she met and married less than two weeks later. Ambitious actress Claire Faulconbridge who plays the scheming heartbreaker in the soap saga, turned her back on Hollywood and superstardom when she laid eyes on

designer Simon Barugh. Five years after their whirlwind courtship they are still happily married . . .

Just the job, says Keith
Keith Evans had a driving ambition – to win a car. And now his dream has come true . . . 'I'm over the moon,' said Keith, 26.

Stop having all these babies, storms Philip
Prince Philip shocked the sexy islanders of a Pacific paradise yesterday by telling them: Stop having so many babies. He blew his top on the sultry Solomon Islands . . . where the loving is easy and big families abound.

Goofed, say girl cops
Gun-toting girl cops Cagney and Lacey are loading up their ammunition to blast the American TV network that axed their highly-rated show.

Gore Blimey
Alan Blood has given his family a shot in the arm . . . by changing their name. After 64 years of cutting jokes spilling out over his unusual surname, Alan persuaded his wife and daughter to agree to the new name of Bloor.

Ex-Angel Erica's a gift from Heaven
No wonder Erica Preston looks like an angel . . . she used to be a children's nurse. The 22-year-old lass from Essex turned to modelling because she thought her job was a little too starchy. We're sure all the kids were sorry to see the back of beautiful Erica . . . but we grown-ups are sure glad to see the front.

News

Headlines

Owen's tough medicine shocks Libs.

Warship races to terror isle.

Sabotage mystery of pilot's dying screams.

Fury as Scargill blows £6000 on luxuries.

Andropov sticks to his guns.

Salvo as Benn bids for poll comeback.

Cigarette ban plan may go up in smoke.

Lebanon bird killing ruffles Israeli feathers.

IRA kiss of death clue to escapes.

Battle lines for common touch.

The Ayatollah writes his new law in blood.

Maggie guns for pin-striped mob.

Danger men's jail 'on brink of bloodbath'.

Can hero Glenn rocket into White House?

Spare Rib caught in Zionist crossfire.

Stories

Furious Zimbabwe Premier Robert Mugabe yesterday blasted Britain for its efforts to have three jailed white air force officers released. Angrily thumping a table, he said he was 'disgusted and dismayed' . . .

We are at war with America over tax – again. This time, though, it is the Americans and their goods who may find themselves dumped in the water. Big British companies are springing to arms against the 13 states who have changed their tax rules to milk the foreign-owned companies. No taxation without representation, they cry.

Christmas is coming and the whisky barons are preparing to do battle over the £150m slice of the home market for Scotch. The salesmen and the marketing chiefs are putting the final touches to their plans for winning a bigger share of spending during Britain's traditional year-end bingo. But they know that by the New Year, some of them will be left nursing a bigger than usual hangover.

105

Phone chaos loomed last night as union bosses warned of lightning walkouts if British Telecom carried out a sacking threat.

Britain's bosses didn't give Mrs Thatcher a lot to smile about at the annual CBI conference. She has never had much love for them as the collective voice of industry. And CBI chief Sir Terence Beckett's clearly intended dig-in-the-chest speech against the government couldn't have pleased her. Clearly, the CBI wants all things for all men.

Heatwave Britain boiled in Mediterranean weather yesterday . . . and the beaches were full of Riviera-style topless girls. As temperatures soared, all over the country some sunlovers got down to the bare essentials.

Shock, horror, scandal!

Headlines

My night of wine and passion.

Witch king in wedding day fury.

Love shock MP flees to hideaway.

Saudi jail hell of flogged Britons.

Pedlars of death trap children in their evil web.

Jekyll and Hyde life of gay TV star.

Did Kennedy hit-man murder Marilyn?

Kinky Sir's spanking kit for bad girls.

Bail rat on run can't hide from Mafia fury.

My sex pervert son, by church minister.

I was the Devil's plaything: orgy caverns haunt Thelma.

Terror reign of jail drug barons.

Head's sexy wife tells her secrets.

Marriage feud girl dies in blaze raid.

Birds and booze ruin supergrass.

Stories

Goings-on in the tiny hamlet of Ashen Grove have led lusty locals to nickname it Passion Grove. Four couples who live in the isolated lane of luxury houses are now involved in divorces after a bewildering bout of partner-swapping. The Kent hot-spot is off East Hill, Otford . . .

Busty Barbara Windsor's heart went out last night to pretty Lorraine Nicklin, the girl Bab's romeo boyfriend planned to wed. 'I could cry for this girl,' said the 46-year-old Carry On star.

Strait-laced bachelor Elgar Jenkins' big secret is out . . . he has a hideaway girlfriend and a love-child. The 47-year-old bespectacled deputy head of a Roman Catholic school has set up Deirdre Church, 33, in a cottage love-nest.

The heartbroken mother of society girl Monika Telling wept last night as she talked for the first time about her daughter's gruesome death.

Out of the corner of her huge, haunted eyes, Princess Elizabeth of Toro gives me an anguished glance as she talks of mass murder, rape and soldiers beating babies to death.

Gunman's girl Sue Stephens clutched a bizarre voodoo charm yesterday – and told of the African tribal chief she believes saved her life. Sexy Sue, 25, was the passionate lover of jailed 'Houdini' David Martin . . .

An armed gang of drug-crazed anarchists are plotting to blaze a trail of terror across Britain. The nomadic wild bunch, up to 500 strong and known as The Tribe, roam the country in convoys of converted lorries, buses and vans and live outside the law.

Sport

Headlines

Albion in goal rush.

Villa withe it!

Lions out like lambs.

Tied up in Notts.

It's red-hot Robbo! Liverpool tame busy bees.

That's for openers!

Gutsy Geoff misses glory by a whisker.

Cruellest cut of all for Butcher.

Rangers wreck wilting Wolves.

Saints go marching on.

Seagulls are still flying.

The England drag act: Robson must quit.

Slick City keep cool.

Painter brushes up Stoke image.

Six of the Best!

Stories

The Brooking-for-England bandwagon is back on the road.

Lunacy? Not after the way he sent Notts County crashing to their fifth successive defeat.

The mystery of the mixed-up match-winner is among the many problems menacing Aston Villa's search for new success in Europe next Wednesday.

Marvellous Marvin Hagler has, as usual, whipped his magnificently muscled body into perfect condition for the defence of his world middleweight title in Las Vegas.

Sue Barker, the one-time golden girl of tennis, tomorrow faces the match she knows will make or break her year.

Schoolgirl Nina Emery played 'truant' yesterday and ended up teaching her rivals a showjumping lesson.

The dazzle and dash of John Woods lifted Leigh to victory yesterday. His silky skills and sizzling speed really put the skids under brave St Helens in an action-packed second half.

Racing's brilliant buccaneer is back and ready to plunder. John Francome, scuppered for nearly three weeks by a crippling kick of fate, sails into action again at Wolverhampton today.

Tell me it's not true. Wake me from the nightmare of a dark, damp night at Wembley, in which England's footballers slowly surrendered to a group of modest Vikings.

Pontypool's remorseless machine took time to clamp into full stride. But when it did, Bridgend were firmly put in their places before the home side again went back into their shells.

Women's World

What if it happened to your daughter?
What happens when the family finds their 16-year-old daughter pregnant? Sandie Laming has been talking to the Lancashire couple for whom it has been the most traumatic event in 22 years of marriage. She has also talked to the girl,

as I sit here in the whisky-ravaged
bar among the tough hard-drinking
war correspondents

Susan, who expects the baby next week. Names have been changed to protect all involved.

Should I leave my wife for this sexy siren's offer?

Dear Barbara, I am serving with the army in Germany and because of a shortage of accommodation my wife and son have to stay in England. I am used to an active sex life and, as I haven't seen my wife for three months, I have found myself getting involved with tourists. One Finnish girl in particular I have been seeing for the last ten days and she has taught me some new things and broadened my outlook on sex. The trouble is . . .

The most way-out woman in town

High society hardly turns a blue-rinsed hair as Jane Kahn walks into the Ritz. But four builders yell enthusiastically from the scaffolding surrounding London's most refined hotel and two policemen stand and stare. Jane Kahn . . . is a walking advert for a way-out trade.

Is your child a genius?

Every mum thinks her child is a genius – and there is a fair chance she could be right. It has been estimated that as many as three babies in every 100 born in Britain could officially be classed as 'gifted'. And they need special treatment from parents and teachers to help them make the most of their brains.

Oh what a beautiful row

The Miss World contest is enjoying its first 'rowover'. From now until the end of the next week, unless organiser Julia Morley is losing her touch, we can expect 'rowovers' to come up at the rate of one every 48 hours. Currently, there is a 'rowover' the girls being monitored by computer and having to complete a test in logical thinking. Protested one girl: 'What has being a beauty queen got to do with computers?' About as little, my lovely, as it has to do with logical thinking.

Hope for families facing drug hell

The 48 people meeting in the large basement room of a London church all had one thing in common. Each one knew the sheer hell of having a drug addict among their nearest and dearest . . .

Sailor-made for elegance
The tweed suit (left) is beautifully tailored. The double-breasted jacket has a neat sailor collar braided in velvet and the skirt is knife-pleated from the hip, which gives a very flattering line.

My husband plays while our home falls apart
Women are often more houseproud than men, who can cheerfully hang their coats on a dirt mark on the wall and not notice when the doors fall off. Unless they fall into their dinners! This could be one root of your problem.

Natasha takes another risk to keep on her toes
Convention has never deterred Natasha Makarova. So when she decided that fulfilment had to come through motherhood she ignored the tradition that ballerinas sacrifice their personal lives for their art . . .

Politics

The origin of politics is lost in the mists of Prime Minister's Question Time. Controversy still rages over how, when and where it first reared its ugly head, but one thing is certain: politics is a murky business. It uses language to cloud rather than clarify. The Gold Standard of meaning has long since been abandoned. Written or spoken, words are the victims of constant Devaluation.

Man is by nature a political animal – or so said Aristotle Onassis, whose ships launched a thousand unacceptable faces. A veteran of the quotable quote, Aristotle gave us some of the earliest recorded clichés. He lived in the home of democracy and the buck stopped there. If he couldn't stand the heat, he got out of the kitchen and cooled himself in the winds of change. Though the business of America was business, he knew that the only thing to fear was fear itself and so he decided he had better wait and see. He understood about peace in our time, and rivers of blood, and spectres haunting Europe, and Cold War diplomacy, and Tory vermin, and Liberty, Fraternity and Equality, and the cult of personality, and the iron hand up the velvet skirt. A natural political animal, he preferred to make love and not water. All in all, he never had it so good.

Considerations of space and threats of libel have tightened the focus of this section to the British political scene. Language there is in a constant state of flux with each party defining the current clichés in different ways. A harmless phrase like 'new blood in the Cabinet' is liable to three main interpretations. Tories will know that their leader has appointed someone under the age of seventy as Chancellor of the Duchy of Lancaster; Labour members will realise that the Premier has ordered transfusions for her more anaemic policies; and Liberals will be certain that Count Dracula has taken over the post of Health Minister. One phrase, three contradictory meanings: such is the charm of politics.

Clichés do not only take the form of words, of course. There are cliché policies, cliché poses and, most familiar of all perhaps, cliché politicians. They are human beings who seem to be Identikit pictures of their respective parties. At the beginning of this century, for instance, the archetypal Tory was Arthur James Balfour. A wealthy patrician educated at Eton and Cambridge, he had one foot in the Victorian age and the other on the golf course. His Liberal counterpart was Herbert Henry Asquith, an industrious Yorkshireman from a poor home who won a scholarship to Oxford and never looked back. As its first MP, Keir Hardie both represented and defined the Labour Party. He was a blunt, fearless, forthright man with a cloth cap and he stood for a Welsh constituency.

Fifty years produced a metamorphosis. The cliché Conservative of our post-war world was Winston Churchill. A wealthy patrician educated at Harrow and Sandhurst, he had one foot in the Victorian Age and the other in Hansard. Liberalism was embodied by Jo Grimond, an industrious man with a faded grandeur who never looked back without asking where his party went wrong. Aneurin Bevan spoke for the Labour Party, a blunt, fearless, forthright man with a cloth cap on all his speeches and a Welsh constituency standing for him. Thus hath the whirligig of time brought in its stereotypes.

In the final analysis, however, politics is a matter of opinion. Parties have a difference of emphasis and it often leads them to a frank interchange of views. MPs are, after all, the guardians of democracy in a country where our representative government is the envy of foreigners – indeed, no other civilised country in the western hemisphere pays quite so much per capita for its politics as Britain. Truly, we get the House of Commons that we deserve.

Parliament is the custodian of our liberties. It is a vineyard of sour grapes in which the wine is always crimson, a football stadium packed with rival fans, a torture chamber for the weak, a pulpit for the strong, a Hall of Mirrors, a Museum of Nine Day Wonders, a hot air sauna, an Arctic gale, a cemetery of noble causes, a junk shop of discarded propaganda, a Garden of Eden in which Adam is still arguing about the price of Golden Delicious. History has come full circle.

Let us now visit our MP at Westminster and have our

photographs taken with him against a background of political clichés . . .

The Conservative Party

Basic Tenets

We are the party of free enterprise.

Ours is the voice of moderation.

Conservatism means a higher standard of living.

Only Tories have the courage to tackle inflation.

The Health Service is safe with us.

Nationalisation does not work. If a nationalised industry breaks this rule by making a substantial profit, we privatise it.

Trade Unions are a threat to the body politic and must be subjugated by law, smear campaigns and justified police brutality.

As the heirs to Disraeli, Baldwin and Churchill, we are the natural party of government.

We propose to rely on the sublime instincts of an ancient people. Help us to make Great Britain truly great once more.

Our record speaks for itself.

Leader

Sex: Female.

Age: Fifties.

Class: Upper middle.

Status: Wife of successful businessman and mother of newsworthy children.

Character:	Patronising in victory and vengeful in defeat.
Poses:	Brittania, the Queen, the Iron Lady, I'm-an-ordinary-housewife-too.
Talent:	Media manipulation and tyrranical control over her party colleagues.
Weakness:	Over-confidence.

MPs

Sex:	Male, female, discreetly gay.
Age:	Fortyish.
Class:	Aspiring upper middle.
Status:	Lawyers, doctors, career women, businessmen, former television personalities, and professional politicians.
Tendency:	Not militant. For Queen, country and capitalism. Treating all opponents with well-dressed contempt. Ambitious, arrogant and complacent. Notorious for extent and profitability of extra-parliamentary activities. Blandly clubbable.
Names:	Nigel, Norman, Mark, Geoffrey, Edward, Margaret, Sally.

Voters

Men:	Establishment Tories, professional classes and furtive, fee-paying trade unionists who read the *Daily Express*. Grass root support from farmers.
Women:	Establishment wives, career women, tweedy ladies in the Home Counties who drive to the

polling station in the second Rover, and the rural vote.

The Party

Strength: Its uncanny ability to survive so long and change so little.

Weakness: High incidence of sex scandals.

Hobbies: Union bashing, Red hunting, and the systematic butchery of former leaders who lost an election.

Myth: Britain is a one-party state.

Tory Jargon

Communists – anyone left of Mussolini.

Soviet Dupes – the Labour Party.

Dogma – a disease from which other parties suffer.

Hustings – a telly interview with Sir Robin Day.

Exile – a political appointment in Northern Ireland.

Top-level talks – a sherry party at Chequers.

A special relationship – an understanding between Ministers and their secretaries.

Pack of lies – statistics which show another sharp rise in unemployment.

Major breakthrough – statistics which can be adjusted to show a tiny fall in unemployment.

New initiatives – old policies retyped.

119

The City – Conservative voters.

A caring society – RSPCA.

Silent minority – the rest of the Cabinet.

Parliament – somewhere to go between board meetings.

Underdeveloped countries – Oh God! Not another bloody debate on Wales and Scotland!

Free Speech

I implore the Government to take very serious note of this issue. It could have disastrous repercussions on the lives of every man, woman, child and illegal immigrant in this country. We must make a stand, be *seen* to make a stand, and, if necessary, sit it out until the bitter end. What is at stake here is nothing less than the future of private enterprise as we know it. The facts are simple: a consortium of Conservative voters has had its application to build a Sewage Farm in the middle of Hackney turned down by the GLC. This is an outright attack on the basic freedoms of the individual. It is outrageous and iniquitous that a profitable scheme like this should be rebuffed for the paltry reason that it will involve a small amount of demolition, forcible rehousing and cosmetic alteration to one of our most revered boroughs. We must fight on the beaches, we must fight in the ballot boxes, we must fight to get served in the House of Commons bar. In the short term, the medium term, and the long term, we are in the business of promoting business. The Hackney Sewage Farm is a watershed in the history of profiteering. We must defend it to the last electoral roll. Our signal is SOS – Save Our Sewage! This, gentlemen, is the stuff of politics!

The Labour Party

Basic Tenets

We are the party of the working classes.

Ours is the voice of reason.

Labour means a higher standard of living for all.

Only socialists have the know-how to beat inflation.

The Health Service was created by us.

Nationalisation always works. If a nationalised industry breaks this rule and runs up enormous losses, we refer to it as an essential public service.

Trade unions are the backbone of society and must be protected from Tory legislation and inquiries into the disposition of their funds.

As the heirs to Attlee, Wilson and Callaghan, we are the natural party of government.

We rely on the good sense of the common people to help us seize control of the means of production, distribution and exchange.

Our record speaks for itself.

Leader

Sex: Male.

Age: Forties.

Class: Limbo between working and middle.

Status: Husband and father.

Character: Welsh in victory and even more Welsh in defeat.

Poses: Nye Bevan, Oliver Cromwell, Max Boyce, As-you-know-me-all-a-plain-blunt-man.

Talent: Fire-in-the-belly eloquence.

Weakness: A sense of humour.

121

MPs

Sex: Male, female, aggressively un-gay.

Age: Fortyish.

Class: Aspiring lower.

Status: Horny-handed sons of the shop floor, lawyers, media refugees and highly-paid professional men who claim their great-grandmothers were Lancashire mill-girls.

Tendency: Militant. For state control and soaking the rich. Treating all opponents with cloth-capped abuse. Assertive, argumentative and scornful. Notorious for the absence and unprofitability of their extra-parliamentary activities. Noisy workingmen's clubbable.

Names: Ted, Joe, Bill, Jack, Tom, Arthur, Jim, Joan, Barbara, Pat.

Voters

Men: Rank and file creatures of habit, students, teachers and trendy intellectuals who take but do not read *The Guardian*. Underground swell of support from miners.

Women: Labour wives, boiler-suited feminists in the provinces, journalists and alternative women who go to the polling station on the number 49 bus.

The Party

Strength: The simplicity of its appeal.

Weakness: Absence of sex scandals.

122

Hobbies:	Millionaire bashing, Nazi hunting, and the religious observance of deadly blood feuds between its members.
Myth:	We are the masters now.

Labour Jargon

Fascists – anyone right of Eric Heffer.

White House Dupes – Conservatives.

Dogma – a lively party game for conferences.

Hustings – addressing a meeting in a church hall in Pontefract attended by two old ladies, a blind man and his dog, and an impatient caretaker.

Exile – appointment as Shadow spokesman on Sport.

Top-level discussions – casual encounter in the chip shop.

A special relationship – Tony Benn and the media.

Pack of lies – anything in the *Daily Telegraph*.

Major breakthrough – apology in the *Daily Telegraph*.

New initiatives – haircuts all round for the Shadow Cabinet.

The City – the local football team.

A caring society – one that votes Labour.

Silent minority – Harold Wilson.

Parliament – somewhere to go between branch meetings.

Underdeveloped countries – chance of a free holiday disguised as an all-party fact-finding visit.

Free Speech

Mark my words, brothers, it's the first step on the slippery slope to rampant capitalism. The vicious increase of 1p on prescription charges in all VD Clinics is a flagrant example of Tory misrule. What about the workers? As one myself, look you, indeed to goodness, boyos, I defend the right of every British citizen to get a dose on the NHS. Don't let them privatise your privates! Ee by gum, it's nobbut a reet scandal. This great Labour Movement was inspired by a vision of free glass eyes. In the teeth of hostile opposition, we strove for free dentures. And who kept the country on its toes with free artificial legs? It's nae guid enough to tell we poor mortals north of the border to pay up. The Tories are not only shafting us, they're charging us for the treatment we need afterwards! It's the rich wot gets the penicillin – ain't it all a bleedin' shame! Unity is strength. At the end of the day, in the white heat of the technological revolution, though cowards flinch and traitors sneer, for the first time in British history, we must invoke the spirit of democratic socialism and make our VD Clinics safe places to walk in after a good night. We Yorkshire lads'll give them a fight. Hands off, Tories! Inject freedom! Vote Labour and nationalise the clap!

The Liberal Party

Basic Tenets

We are the party of true radicalism.

Ours is the voice of reasonable moderation.

Liberalism means higher standards.

Only Liberals have the audacity to criticise the way that others tackle inflation.

We created the preconditions for the creation of the Health Service.

Nationalisation does not work unless humanised by Liberal values.

Trade Unions are both the backbone of society and a threat to the body politic. We intend to have a policy on them in due course.

As the heirs to Gladstone, Asquith and Lloyd George, we are the natural party of government.

We appeal to the middle ground of the nation which is fed up with the farce of two-party politics.

Our record speaks for itself.

Leader

Sex:	**Male.**
Age:	Forties.
Class:	Middle.
Status:	Lawyer, husband, father.
Character:	Dourly Scots in defeat. Not acquainted with victory so far.
Poses:	The Conscience of Britain, Rob Roy, the Boy Wonder. Pull-the-other-one-Jimmy!
Talent:	Photogenic and kind to old ladies.
Weakness:	Takes long and inconvenient holidays.

MPs

Sex:	Male, female, we did warn you.
Age:	Indeterminate.
Class:	Middling.
Status:	Lawyers, businessmen, cookery writers.

Tendency:	Towards frustration because of their lack of influence. Treating opponents with liberal disdain. Ambitious, anti-authoritarian, alliance-conscious. Notorious for the extent and unprofitability of their election appearances. Limited clubbability.
Names:	David, Cyril, Russell.

Voters

Men:	Old-style Liberals, malcontents from other parties, small businessmen.
Women:	Wives of old-style Liberals. Career women. Middle-of-the-roaders.

The Party

Strength:	Resilience in the face of repeated disappointments at the polls.
Weakness:	Lloyd George knew its father.
Hobbies:	Tory bashing, Red hunting and constant public self-definition.
Myth:	When Liberals come to power . . .

Liberal Jargon

Reds and Fascists – those who do not vote Liberal or SDP.

Dupes – the incumbent government.

Dogma – something that will come in time.

Hustings – cars, helicopters, buses, shopping precincts when the telly cameras are there.

Exile – being a Liberal in the House of Lords.

Top-level talks – Get me the SDP on the 'phone!

A special relationship – Jeremy Thorpe and Norman Scott.

Pack of lies – opinion polls showing Liberal decline.

Major breakthrough – stopping Cyril Smith from becoming the Deputy Leader.

New initiatives – why don't we devise a policy on Inflation?

The City – as opposed to the country.

A caring society – has proportional representation.

Silent minority – the Parliamentary party.

Parliament – somewhere to go when it rains.

Underdeveloped countries – pass me that atlas, please.

Free Speech

I welcome this golden opportunity to speak to you, here, today, in the canteen of this zip-fastener factory in Walsall, on the eve of the most epoch-making General Election in the history of British politics. Let me begin by nailing the lie that the Liberal Party has no aim and policy. Our aim has always been – to find a policy. Meanwhile, we have a prepared statement on everything from Monetarism to Meths Drinking, including a footnote on the strange similarity between the two of them. People ask us, for instance, where we stand on Northern Ireland. Gladstone made our position abundantly clear, I feel. As for Protectionism, who could improve on the words of Asquith, Liberal Prime Minister, statesman, and writer of love letters to the charming Venetian Stanley Baldwin? The Liberal Party has taken a distinctive stance from the start and it has alarmed medical men. As for nuclear disarmament, there is, alas, no recorded comment in Lloyd

George's Diary (apart from pencilled jottings about sudden explosions and going naked into the conference chamber) on the subject. In short, we take a neutral position, such as we occupied during the Franco-Prussian War. A vote for the Liberals is a protest vote against two monolithic parties. It is a vote for decency, for commonsense, for radical democracy and for all the values that any civilised country holds dear. At the last election nine out of ten people voted Liberal but, owing to the callous inequalities of our electoral system, only a handful of our candidates won seats. It has been predicted that, with proportional representation, the Liberal Party would have had two and a half more seats and several square yards of standing room in the Strangers' Gallery. Finally, to the question that I am always asked. The answer is that *we* broke the mould before they did. If I may quote Sir Henry Campbell-Bannerman . . .

The Social Democratic Party

Basic Tenets

We are the party of free enterprise, the working classes, and true radicalism.

Ours is the voice of weason and modewation.

SDP means Some Day Please . . .

Only SDP members have the bravery to reject Courage, with its inflationary effects, in favour of claret.

We are safe with the Health Service.

Nationalisation does not work. In case it does, we have a policy to meet that contingency as well.

Trade Unions are a threat to the backbone unless they form a united front with us.

As the heirs to Social Democracy, we are the natural party of government.

We propose to rely on the occasional freak by-election to keep us in the public eye.

If we had one, our record would speak for itself.

Leader

Sex: Male.

Age: Forties.

Class: Middle.

Status: Doctor, husband, father.

Character: Seasoned in defeat, an unknown quantity in victory.

Poses: Foreign Secretary, Flash Harry, the Bostick of the Alliance. Love-me-love-my-bedside-manner.

Talent: Unhurried opportunism and smiling plausibility.

Weakness: Over-intelligent.

MPs

Sex: Male.

Age: Fortyish and upwards.

Class: Bang in the middle.

Status: Professional politicians who have burned their boats.

Tendency: Neither to right nor left. Pro this, that and the other. Treating opponents with educated hostility. Ambitious, ambidextrous and pioneering. Notorious for the extent and suddenness of their betrayals of former parliamentary colleagues. As clubs go, number 2 irons.

Names: David, Ian, Bill, Roy.

Voters

Men: Right-wing socialists and left-wing Tories, plus middle-of-the-roaders who had given up the Liberals as a lost cause.

Women: Professional women, disenchanted dropouts from other parties, bandwagoners.

The Party

Strength: Its novelty value.

Weakness: Inexperience and lack of definition.

Hobbies: Being matey with each other, talking about breaking the mould of British politics, prick-teasing the Liberals.

Myth: As the only credible alternative party . . .

SDP Jargon

The common enemy – former parliamentary colleagues.

Dupes – those who vote for other parties.

Dogma – anything quoted in *The Guardian*.

Hustings – well-publicised walkabouts in busy provincial cities.

Exile – spokesman on immigration.

Top-level talks – David and David (Brokers) Ltd.

A special relationship – Woy, David, Shirley and Bill.

Pack of lies – any criticism of the SDP.

Major breakthrough – any criticism of the SDP that can be turned to account.

New initiatives – latest intake from other parties.

The City – policy document on urban renewal.

A caring society – British Wine Association.

Silent minority – deposed SDP MPs.

Parliament – somewhere to go past occasionally.

Underdeveloped countries – those without SDP Parties.

Free Speech

A love affair is a long time in politics. The Duke of Wellington (the Iron Poker of Whitehall) told romance to publish and be damned. Palmerston, gunboat diplomat, favoured short, sharp, navel engagements. Disraeli made women dizzy. A certain Liberal premier knew my father and just about everyone's mother. Sir John Profumo told another tale – well, he would, wouldn't he? And in recent years more than one House of Commons secretary has learned the horrid truth. Do not trust Tory erection promises: they lead to Labour pains. Out of this sordid morass of deceit and detumescence has come a genuine love story to warm the cockles of the electorate's heart. Boy meets girl: Liberal meets SDP. Passion blends with romance, and animal vigour comes to terms with yearning nostalgia. It is the greatest marriage of true minds since Agriculture and Fisheries. And out of this unbridled desire, a new child – the Alliance – is born. It was conceived by a gang of Four Fathers, and dedicated to the proposition that all men are created equal in the sight of the Returning Officer. There have been disagreements, lovers' tiffs, momentary errors of misunderstanding, but they have been ignored by the proud parents. The Alliance is a bouncing baby who takes up several seats in the House. When his teething troubles are over, he will spread himself even more. Vote SDP and endorse a love affair. Give generously and receive rewards of the heart. Then social democracy of the people, by the people, and for the people of Hillhead shall not perish.

Minority Parties

Minority parties are major institutions to the people in them. No matter how small they may be, they are sustained by the same big dream of power. When the great day dawns, they believe, the Flat Earthers, the Gay Liberation Falangists, the Reigate Christian Militia and Women Hairdressers Against The Bomb will take over. Parliament will become the plaything of the Wolverhampton Workers' Revolutionary Reggae Group. Shortly before her execution, the Queen will invite the League of Redundant Fishmongers to form a government. Conservationists from the Save-Our-Shropshire-Canals Campaign will barge into the Stock Exchange and the rebel leader of the Gas Consumers Council for Peace in Europe will be appointed as chairman of British Rail. Even a Catastrophe Party can look at a king.

For a country which prides itself on its studied apathy to politics, Britain has produced an amazing crop of minority parties. They surface from the soil during every by-election and blossom in the sunlight of a week's publicity. The ballot box soon harrows them and they vanish beneath the land of lost deposits, only to sprout up again at the next opportunity. It only takes three people and a mischievous sense of humour to form a minority party and so they grow in vast numbers.

Movement between them is constant and they change their names with confusing regularity.

Because there are far too many of them to look at individually, this study must restrict itself to four of the major minority parties. Each has been on the fringe of British politics for some time now and all of them embody the hopes and fears of the smaller unit. Here is a cliché guide to:

The Communist Party – roads to freedom.
The National Front – keep the Black Country white.
Plaid Cymru – the leek shall inherit the earth.
Scottish Nationalist Party – campaign for lead-free whisky.

Be nice to the minority party. They are the variety that provides the spice on the political scene.

The Communist Party

Basic Tenets

Comrades – man is born free yet everywhere he is in chains.

Comrades – socialism is the only way to solve our problems.

Comrades – we must end class divisions in our society.

Comrades – we must take political power from the grasping hands of an exploitive capitalist minority.

Comrades – we demand a planned economy based on socialist principles, and aimed at improving the living and working conditions of the people.

Comrades – we demand socialist nationalisation of industry, banks, insurance companies, distributive monopolies, land, the media and the Royal Family.

Comrades – we demand the strengthening and extension of all democratic rights, and measures to ensure the just administration of socialist law.

Comrades – we demand that Britain be made strong, free and independent, with a foreign policy of peace and friendship with all nations.

Comrades – we demand that you realise the message of our programme is one of hope and confidence. The working people, acting together, can seize political power, by force if need be, and so end the exploitation of man by man, and Tory Party by woman. We demand that the people build a Socialist Britain in which everyone not imprisoned is happy and in which society is organised on the principle that 'the free development of each is the condition of all, Comrades.'

Comrades – we demand . . .

Comrades . . .

Communist Jargon

Freedom – freedom to vote for the Communist Party in a Communist Britain and to take part in the May Day Parade every fortnight, Comrade.

Culture – a remake of *Reds* starring Arthur Scargill, and a never-ending television drama series based on the novels of Karl Marx.

Trots – any political extremist expelled from the Communist Party.

Labour Movement – every man, woman and child in the country who is not a paid official of the ruling Communist hierarchy.

Capital – a source of inequality and power that has now been captured and taken over by the Communist Party who use it instead as a source of Communist inequality and Communist power.

Democracy – a quaint item on display in the Black Museum.

Class traitors – anyone who dares to complain because three families have to share a single room in the new high-rise blocks of workers' flats around Trafalgar Red Square.

Confrontation – a visit to the cells to account for any deviation from Communist principles – such as taking one's holiday in Majorca instead of such prescribed paradises as Central Siberia or war-torn Afghanistan.

Education – I believe in God, the Father Almighty, maker of Marx and Engels, and in V I Lenin, His son, who was conceived by sub-committee, born of Virgin Soil, and who taught us how to break the cruel monopoly of capitalist barbers . . .

Foreign Policy – Hello, is that Moscow 123, Comrade . . .?

The National Front

Basic Tenets

Man is born free yet everywhere he is living next door to a Pakistani.

Nationalism and Patriotism are the only solutions to our problems.

We must end racial divisions in our society by shipping out Blacks, Packs and other foreigners.

We must seize political power and exercise it for our own partisan purposes.

We demand a National Front economy based on true Fascist principles, and aimed at ruining the living and working conditions of the people.

We demand totalitarianism so that the owners of industry, banks, insurance companies, distributive monopolies, land, the media and the Royal Family will have no fear of declaring their allegiance to Fascist policies. Special purges will remove Leftist sympathisers from such programmes as News at Ten, World in Action *and* Jackanory.

We demand a huge increase in the penalties for such crimes as internationalism, racial integration and miscegenation.

We demand that Britain be made strong, free, independent, whiter-than-white, and that her foreign policy be one of outright aggression against all other countries.

We demand that you join us in unity – the unity that comes of dedication to great common faith. You have all seen the hate that we engender in our enemies, a hate that neither Labour nor Conservative members encounter. That hate is the surest sign of our success and our potential. We demand a Fascist Britain in which society is organised on the principle that 'free development of hatred is the way to love and understanding.'

Keep Britain red, white and blue . . .

Keep Britain . . .

National Front Jargon

Freedom – freedom to attack and persecute racial minorities without any interference from the forces of law and order.

Culture – mandatory poetry readings from *Mein Kampf* and a rock opera based on the life and aims of Sir Oswald Mosley – *The Destiny of Force*.

Trots – anybody without a swastika tattooed on their chest.

Labour Movement – controlled deployment of working people to the camps in the country where they are most needed.

Capital – a London radio station that will be immediately commandeered so that Fascist propaganda can be played between the pop records.

Democracy – a notifiable disease.

137

Class Traitors – a person who aids, abets or otherwise condones racial minorities who try to escape compulsory repatriation. Class traitors will be liable to imprisonment or transportation.

Confrontation – regular Saturday afternoon battles with any remaining Wogs or Lefties to be held in White City Stadium to the music of the British national anthem. Results will be announced on Sports Report and League Tables kept up-to-date.

Education – Hitler Youth Camps for teenagers and national Rehabilitation Centres for older people who have not been fully indoctrinated with the values of a Fascist government. Uniform will be worn at all times and drill is enforced.

Foreign Policy – splendid isolation with regard to America and the Common Market countries. Vigorous friendship with all white nations in the British Empire; expulsion of all black nations from the Empire. Standing army kept in readiness at all times to defend Queen and Country.

Plaid Cymru

Basic Tenets

All Welshmen are born free yet everywhere you look we've got the bloody English!

National self-determination is the only solution to our problems.

We must end class and racial divisions by driving the English back over the border.

We must seize political power from the grasping hands of Parliament and devolve of our own volition.

We demand a Welsh economy based on weaving, coal-mining and coracle-making, and aimed at enriching the living and working conditions of the people.

We demand nationalisation of Welsh industry, banks, insurance companies, distributive monopolies, land, the media, sheep and reservoirs. Instead of gushing away by the gallon into English gullets, Welsh water will be bottled and sold as a healthful beverage.

We demand a huge increase in the penalties for kicking, biting in the scrum, deliberate obstruction and losing to any visiting English teams.

We demand that Wales be made free, strong, totally independent, and that her foreign policy be one of choral harmony with other countries.

We demand a Free Wales in which life is one long Eisteddfod with prizes for everyone. We support Home Rule for Harry Secombe and will instigate extradition procedures to return Tom Jones, Shirley Bassey and Cliff Morgan to the land of their fathers. Welsh coinage will replace existing currency. The franked head of the Queen will be replaced by that of an old goat – with thanks to the descendants of Lloyd George for their permission. Society will be organised on the principle that 'the free development of Wales is the precondition of happiness'.

We'll keep a welcome in the hillsides . . .

We'll keep . . .

Plaid Cymru Jargon

Freedom – the amount of room given to an outside-half by the opposing flank forwards.

Culture – copies of *the Mabinogion*, instead of the Gideon Bible, in all lonely hotel rooms. Musical version of *How Green Was My Valley*, complete with choir of singing pit ponies, will tour the Rhondda.

Trots – you would have that second helping of gooseberry pie, mun!

Labour movement – decision to have the next baby at a maternity hospital in Llanelli.

Capital – Cardiff. The seat of government in the People's

139

Republic of Wales. All streets and roads will be renamed after Druids or members of the Grand Slam Team of 1977-8; and Cardiff Castle will become the official residence of the new President of Wales.

Democracy – electing a new captain for Pontypool RFC.

Class traitors – Welshmen with holiday cottages in England, and pupils who show up their colleagues by learning the homework set.

Confrontation – getting back late and drunk yet again from the Club and finding the wife waiting.

Education – export of teachers to England to cease at once. All education to be bilingual and to be based on the principle of **Cymru Am Byth**. Every schoolbook to be bound in red so that we can have no more **Brad Y Llyfrau Gleision** (Treachery of the Blue Books). New Welsh-slate Universities to be built in every county. Compulsory education until the age of 35 unless exempted by service in the Welsh National Army or in the tenor section of the Morriston Orpheus.

Foreign Policy – always take the game to them. Put them under pressure, harry them into mistakes, control the second phase, then work the ball out to Gerald on the wing.

Scottish National Party

Basic Tenets

Scotsmen are born free – but there's a wee surcharge for the lassies.

Home Rule is the only way to solve our insolvency.

We must end class divisions and make Hampden Park into an all-seating stadium.

We must wrest political power from the manicured fingers of the Sassenach and control our own destiny again.

We demand a completely unplanned economy based on SNP

principles, and aimed at maximising the joy of the average Glaswegian by extending opening hours.

We demand nationalisation of all basic resources in Scotland, including the North Sea oilfield. We repudiate the sovereignty of the Queen and the Duke of Edinburgh and appoint, in their places, Lulu and Rod Stewart.

We demand the strengthening of all democratic rights, and a more stringent supervision of what goes into a haggis.

We demand that Scotland be made strong, free, totally independent and allowed to travel on Football Specials to Wembley. Our foreign policy, like our bagpipes, will be played by ear.

We demand a new deal for the Scottish people who have been in the shadow of Whitehall for far too long. Edinburgh will henceforth be known as the Athens of the North; Glasgow as the Chicago of the East; Aberdeen as the Murmansk of the South; and Dundee as Cake City. We demand that a self-governing, self-controlled, self-service Scotland be built as a challenge to the Tesco Empire. Oil revenues will be used to improve public facilities and to redecorate the Home for Retired Caber Tossers. Society will be organised so that there is everything on Scottish soil. Kenny Dalgleish, Charlie Nicholas and other exiles will be repatriated at once; Billy Connolly will be the new Rock of Scone. A referendum will be held on the problem of what to do with Sheena Easton.

Is there anything back on the empties, Jimmy?

Scottish Nationalist Jargon

Freedom – the wearing of the kilt (Ah, that's better!)

Culture – Burns Night every second Friday and a McHammer McHorror Film version of *Brigadoon* entitled *Meg Brockie and the Beastie of Lammermoor*, and starring Noele Gordon and Ronnie Corbett.

Trots – journeys to the off-licence.

Labour Movement – Eh, will y' wake up there, lads, here comes the soddin' foreman again!

Capital – money kept in a tartan sock under the loose floorboard in the bedroom, and saved for a rainy day with the au pair girl,

Democracy – the inalienable right of every Scotsman to put his fist through the television screen when the Scottish World Cup Squad is announced and his favourite player has been omitted.

Class traitors – people who insist on reading *The Scotsman* instead of *The McSun*.

Confrontation – standing as SNP candidate in a by-election at Millwall South-East.

Education – free with two milk bottle tops, a wrapper from a packet of shortcake and a signed photograph of Andy Irvine. Compulsory till the age of 10. Special training will be given in the use of the dirk and claymore, and all pupils will take a turn at patrolling the Scottish frontier in case of invasion by the English. New tartan brick universities will be built at Mull, Kelso and Wick. A monster swimming pool will be created in Loch Ness. Pupils who fail their examinations will be sentenced to a season's continuous viewing of the Pitlochry Festival.

Foreign Policy – No fraternising with the English. Fuck their lassies – but don't say thank you!

Professions

The origin of the profession is lost in the mists of time and a half. From the moment that Karl Marx invented the working classes in the Reading Room of the British Museum, there have been vicious demarcation disputes about where the occupation ends and the profession begins. Is landscape gardening a profession? How do you classify funeral directors? What price publishing? A simple rule of thumb is to look at a person who is thrust into the outer darkness of unemployment. The professional man or woman will telephone a friend; the non-professional will visit the Job Centre. The former views work as belonging to an exclusive club while the latter sees it as a means of paying the mortgage. Professional Associations safeguard the one and Trade Unions fight tooth and nail for the other. The dividing line between them is drawn by snobbery.

For definition and guidance we are bound to look to the oldest profession. Made up of people who have achieved a high level of competence in their special area, it operates restricted entry ('Fifty quid a time, sir'), has its own professional lingo ('Hello, sailor. Got a light?') and functions in standardised business premises ('The bed is next door'). For many a jaded client ('You mean, it happens to *other* men as well?') it is truly one of the learned professions. Quality control is high and guarantees of full satisfaction are established practice. For the nervous punter there is even a protective clause ('There's a packet of them in the top drawer, love'). Based on partnerships and offering a confidential service in nocturnal privacy, the oldest profession embodies the criteria of success. Only those that really make it can describe themselves as professionals.

This ruling from on high immediately invalidates such pseudo-professions as accountancy, antique dealing and acting. Would you cruise along a kerb in the red-light district in order to pick up an accountant? How much joy could you expect if you were sitting in the back of a parked car with an expert on French porcelain? With actors, of course, you are always likely to get a clap at the end of a good performance. No, these are not true professions. Their members – along with estate agents, stockbrokers, public relations consultants, journalists, insurance agents, sociologists, philosophers, writers and other Old Pretenders – must be considered as belonging to glorified occupations. Computer programming – a *profession*! Let us observe some strict standards here. There is no easy virtue. At all times we must be sure to weigh the pros against the cons.

When all is said and done, not to beat about the bush, taking everything into account, come hell or high water, as the saying is, in the judgement of their peers, by and large at a loose end, there are only three other professions whose status is universally recognised and whose credibility is above reproach. The Law, the Church, Medicine. These three – but the greatest of them is a matter of legal dispute, constant prayer, and major surgery. Our learned professions. Fortified castles into which only the privileged may enter. Rarefied atmospheres in which only the person with the proper credentials can breathe. Domains of wonder in which magic is worked by means of summons, sermons and sick bays.

The Law exists to regulate society in its every motion. It can be civil to you or downright criminal. It can act as a prevention, a deterrent, a punishment, even, occasionally, as a help. The Church, by contrast, is concerned with the spiritual welfare of its congregation. It may be high or low, plain or fancy, but it shares the same caretaker. Medicine is merely a garage on the highway of life. You pull in every so often for a change of oil or for a full service and then drive on towards the final scrap-yard. The Law saves property, the Church saves souls, and Medicine saves lives. We are prisoners of geometry. The Eternal Triangle encloses us all sooner or later. There is no known escape.

Lack of time holds us back from anything but a brief look at the Law, a cursory glance at the Church, and a summary autopsy on Medicine. But if you will be silent in court, reverent in the house of the Lord, and perfectly still on the operating table, we will proceed. The learned professions have indeed an enormous amount to teach the lay public – which brings us back to the oldest profession once more!

The Law

Born with the faint defects of age, the law has now reached such an advanced stage of senility that it resembles a vast geriatric ward. It is full of archaic forms, tired clichés, sagging euphemisms, moribund technicalities and the eternal, mumbling, meaningless repetition of the incurably ga-ga. Torts wear trusses. Equity needs an enema. Prolixity has a prolapse. The High Court uses a hearing-aid. Quips, quiddities and quillets speak with quavering voices. The bowels of the Statute Book suffer from judicial separation.

Out of deference to the frailty all around them regular visitors wear dark robes, grey wigs and frowns of concentration in order to look older. Grounds of appeal lie in the distant past. Punishments are meted out in terms of time. Palsied eld is everywhere. If it had a good solicitor, the law could sue life for breach of contract.

A major cause of the decay has been the Latinism and it is in evidence on all sides. The law operates in the Accusative Case. It distinguishes between the Active and the Passive, and imprisons Irregular Verbs. It has special courts to deal with Genitive Crimes and will always take into account a defendant's Past Participle. It raises bail by Declension and divorces people by Conjugation, awarding them an Ablative Absolute. In most of its dealings, the Vocative dominates. As befits a dying creature, it talks largely in a dead language.

The cliché characters of the legal world do not seem to change overmuch. Though the brutal policeman ('The accused threw himself repeatedly at the end of my truncheon . . .') is now an established fact, his comical counterpart ('I was proceeding in a northerly direction . . .') is still the norm. The cliché solicitor remains the grey-haired man in the dark suit who occupies an office designed by Charles Dickens. And the average courtroom features the whimsical judge, the officious clerk, the posturing barristers and a jury that looks like a cross-section of the cemetery. Gilbert and Sullivan are still prisoners at the bar; unfortunately, the clichés are no longer set to music.

Cliché Jargon

Conveyancing – the art of slow motion.

Guilty but insane – M'Naughton Rules OK.

Miscarriage of justice – we lost the case.

Quality of mercy – only beaten up the once in police custody.

These things take time – motto of the Law Society.

Harsh sentence – life imprisonment with regular visits by Lord Longford and by makers of television documentaries.

Inadmissible Evidence – I don't care *what* your grandmother's informant thought she heard the milkman say a friend of a friend almost saw through a keyhole in the accused's house.

Diminished responsibility – in passing sentence on you, I shall bear in mind the fact that you were on holiday in the Lake District at the time when the victim was stabbed to death in Ramsgate . . .

Full majesty of the law – when the judge has his robes dry-cleaned, his wig re-dressed, and his obiter dicta polished in the hope of getting press attention.

Softly, softly – after intensive inquiries lasting some eight centuries and more, I arrest you for the Murder of Thomas Becket. Anything you say . . .

How do you plead? – I didn't verbal those fucking verbals!

Hanged in error – and he was such a good chaplain.

Law reform – mouth-to-mouth resuscitation.

The Cross-Examination

A Great Train Robber is cross-examined by Counsel for the Prosecution.

Counsel:	Reggie Biggs of Crippen Cottage, Ten Rillington Place, Acid Bath Fields, The Moors – are you the party of the first part who attended the party in the first part of the evening at the Party Headquarters where you worked part-time at first?
Biggs:	Not guilty!
Counsel:	Can you account for your movements on the date in question?
Biggs:	I went twice.
Counsel:	You were apprehended by a constable, drunk and disorderly –
Judge:	The officer's condition is immaterial.
Counsel:	And you said – I quote – 'It's a fair cop, guv. You got me bang to rights. I'll come quietly. I think our policemen are wonderful.' Is that an accurate record?
Biggs:	It's a frame-up! You got nothing on me!
Counsel:	Members of the Jury, I leave you to draw your own conclusions from the defendant's statement.
Judge:	What about the man on the Clapham omnibus?
Biggs:	Never seen him before in my life!
Counsel:	M'lud, I offer Exhibit A to the court. I put it to you that this is a prima facie case.
Judge:	It looks like imitation leather, at first sight.
Biggs:	I demand a re-trial on the grounds of compassion!

149

Counsel: It is a cornerstone of British justice that a person must be presumed innocent until proven guilty. However, in the case of the Man in the Dock – hereinafter referred to as The Culprit – I believe that we should return to a more ancient and effective legal practice. The Culprit should be taken from this court and hanged by the neck until he confesses to this heinous crime. I rest my case because my arm is aching.

Biggs: You can't pin this on me. I've got an alibi. I've got lots of alibis. One for each member of the jury. And being left-handed, as your ballistics expert has pointed out, I could not possibly have dealt the murder blow.

Counsel: What about that diesel engine found under a tarpaulin in your garden? You stole it from British Rail! Admit it!

Biggs: I was rather hoping you wouldn't bring that up . . .

The Church

> Cliches bright and beautiful,
> Trite phrases great and small,
> Worn words wise and wonderful,
> The Church has got them all.

Christianity has preached the same message for almost two thousand years. Repetition has dulled its impact and time has lessened its importance in the general scheme of things, but you can still find it everywhere. It sings behind the stained glass windows and beneath the vaulted roofs of cathedrals. It shivers on hard wooden benches in stone-flagged, tomb-cold parish churches. It stands bored and resentful in echoing halls during a thousand morning assemblies. Royal marriages show it at its best; wars of religion expose it at its worst. It has a feast day at Christmas.

Uniformed Christianity plays in a brass band in the public

street. Roman Catholicism prefers worship with a touch of Grand Opera. The Society of Friends recommends the personalised earthquake. Welsh Nonconformity fills its chapels with fire and passion. Scottish Presbyterianism exemplifies the virtues of self-denial and the banning of the bagpipes. Seventh Day Adventists make no bones about their Day of Rest. And in dozens of other places the identical Word is spoken in dozens of different ways – at the Bethel Evangelical Church, among the Methodists, Baptists, Unitarians and Christadelphians, in the Lutheran Congregation and the Pentecostal Assembly, in the Spiritualist Sects and the Missionary Organisations, among Jehovah's Witnesses and Christian Scientists and United Reformists, and at the Chapel of the Church of Jesus Christ of Latter-Day Saints. Mormons mormonise.

This glut of God-bothering tends towards religion by numbers. Twelve disciples. Ten commandments. Thirty-nine Articles. Eight Beatitudes. Four Gospels. One Hundred and Fifty Psalms. Seven Days. Three Kings. The Holy Trinity. Into the ark of the Church the animals go two by two in orderly procession – Adam and Eve, Cain and Abel, Samson and Delilah, David and Jonathan, Daniel and the Lion, Mary and Joseph, the bishop and the actress. Christianity is the sum of all human experience.

Cliché Jargon

Act of God – Patience Strong.

A moveable feast – an African missionary chased by a cannibal.

State of Grace – too much Communion wine.

Sexagesima Sunday – make love for Jesus!

Moral Rearmament – mending the holes in one's cassock.

The new theology – the old theology rendered into modern English and thereby deprived of any resonance, authority, magic or hope of getting a laugh.

Mothers' Union – lesbianism in the vestry.

Judgement Day – Manchester United 66. Vatican Wanderers 0.

Benefit of clergy – we shall now take a collection.

Soul in torment – a man forced to read the Gideon Bible in its entirety in the bedroom of a two-star hotel in Sunderland.

Gloria in excelsis – what usually happens if she's *in flagrante* long enough.

The God slot – the vicar's letterbox.

Excommunication – How I Escaped Roman Catholicism.

Decent burial – a generous tip for the gravedigger.

Laying on of hands – the actress and the bishop during morning service.

The Sermon

As we are gathered here in the sight of the Lord, let me commend to you the words of Matthew 8: 21-27; Mark 10: 15-19; Luke 16: 4-9; and John 22: 6-60. Many are called but few are chosen. Consider the lilies of the field. Blest are the pure in heart. I come before you as a Good Shepherd but I am no worker of miracles. Give me some loaves and a few fishes and all I can make is sardine sandwiches. And yet I say unto you, that Solomon in all his glory was not arrayed like Danny La Rue. Hear what comfortable words the Saviour says in Proverbs 3: 90-94; Exodus I: 17-23; and Joshua 37: 55-57. In asking you to give generously to the Home for Retired Joke Vicars, I would beg you to play the Samaritan and not walk past on the other side of the street. Fight the good fight with all your might and do unto others in such a way that they won't do it unto you again in a hurry. I am glad to announce the amalgamation of the Girl Guides with the Boy Scouts – all things proceed to a joyful consummation. A sudden vacancy has occurred for five wise virgins. I urge you to repent in the manner prescribed in Genesis 15: 7-8; and to save your soul after the Ezekiel 12: 41-42 fashion. For there is more joy in heaven over one sinner that repenteth than in ninety-nine sheep who are safe in the fold. May I remind, please, that the Golden Years Annual Outing will take place on Ascension Day when we shall be going down to the valley of the shadow of death and returning before nightfall by way of Damascus. For such of you as are of riper years and yet have undergone public baptism, I look upon you as confirmed friends. For Jesus Christ walked upon water but when he turned it to wine he did the dog-paddle instead. Nowhere is this more clear than in Paul's Epistle to the Guardian Women page. Verily, I say unto you, remember the advice given in Psalm 2: 11-18; and Psalm 4: 26-28. The Church is one foundation and all contributions to its upkeep will be gratefully received. It may be the correct moment to inform you that I will be absent from this pulpit for a short while when I take my holidays, but I expect to be back from the wilderness in forty days and forty nights. With regard to the Bible Study Class, therefore, I would exhort you all to read Matthew, Mark, learn, and inwardly digest the New Testament. In conclusion, I ask you to share in this service of Christian commitment as I read out the remaining hymns, ancient and modern: 312, 675, 444 and – unlucky for some – 13.

Bingo!

Medicine

The medical profession makes clichés of us all. It reduces the most unusual and individual of us to a list of symptoms. We become just another patient with just another clinical history taken into just another hospital for just another routine operation. Everything moves towards the commonplace. Stereotypical attitudes surround us and white-coated jargon subdues us. The process begins before we are even born and continues until the moment that the death certificate is signed. Medicine anaesthetises mankind. We lie helpless beneath its scalpel as it cuts us down to size. The most that we can aspire to be is just one more statistic in the dialogue between pain and its cure. We are 'cases'.

Cliché personnel dominate the profession. They wear the same clothes, the same colours, the same shoes, the same hairstyles, the same spectacles, and the same expressions of dismay in the face of NHS cuts. Normalisation is the norm but the clichés do sometimes undergo plastic surgery. The cliché doctor used to be a wild, irresponsible, irrepressible sex maniac, who, after years of neglecting his studies at medical school in favour of a life of rampant hedonism, somehow passed his examinations with flying colours and became, at a stroke, a pillar of rectitude and an eternal credit to his stethoscope. Today's cliché doctor is more likely to be a Pakistani houseman in a Wolverhampton casualty unit, a brisk, bosomy female GP with firm views on contraception, or a trendy, liberal, Porsche-driving medical expert, who supplements his meagre pittance by writing a column for a women's magazine and answering anguished questions from troubled readers who now wish that they hadn't. Either way, the doctor remains a cliché authority figure in a crumbling world.

The cliché nurse, of course, will always be that strange amalgam of angel and whore that makes her so irresistible to her lecherous superiors and to writers of television drama serials. Hospitalisation helps the image. All nurses look the same when viewed from a bed. Cliché fantasies dent many a male pillow and deflect the mind from the reality of the bedpan. Cliché jokes get plucky patients through difficult days. Cliché diets nourish them and restore them and make them fit for discharge. Cliché pills keep them alive and kicking until the final cliché kills them.

Cliché Jargon

First Aid – take two aspirins and call me in the morning.

Nutritional disorder – when did your husband discover that he *liked* the taste of imported Korean furniture?

Placebo – drink this coloured water three times a day. And don't worry about having bubonic plague – there's a lot of it about.

Schizophrenia – a condition that is bad for both of you.

Blood pressure – the speed at which it spurts out under the surgeon's knife.

Disputed diagnosis – okay, so *you* think it's fluid on the knee, and *I* say it's heart disease. Couldn't we meet each other halfway and tell the poor bugger he's got a hernia?

Unforeseen side effects – try not to be alarmed about it, Mrs Henshaw. Once we get the drug balance right, you'll soon stop laying free range eggs.

Family planning – and then in May, 1988, we'd like a boy, around 7lbs, who prefers to be bottle-fed, sleeps through the night, and grows up with a healthy respect for his parents . . .

Appointments system – I intend to book you in for a series of house calls, Mrs Raver. Now, *when* did you say your husband was on the night shift . . .?

Hippocratic oath – sworn by every doctor who inadvertently stitches two of his own fingers together.

Freudian aberration – Sigmund, what are you *doing* in those fish-net tights!

The kiss of life – the stage that comes after the bedside manner.

Second opinion – excuse me, but shouldn't we have taken off her *other* leg instead?

The Consultation

A patient visits a doctor for a routine check-up.

Doctor: You can get dressed now, Mr Watts. I'll just put this torch and magnifying glass away. (**He does so and picks up pad**). Now, I want to ask you a few questions to keep my records up to date . . . How many notifiable diseases have you had?

Patient:	None.
Doctor:	Minor illnesses?
Patient:	None.
Doctor:	Fractures, dislocations, bruises?
Patient:	None.
Doctor:	Have you never cut yourself shaving?
Patient:	Never.
Doctor:	Any mental disturbance in your family?
Patient:	None – apart from a great aunt who likes *Dallas*.
Doctor:	Operations, referrals, treatment as an out-patient?
Patient:	None.
Doctor:	You must have been on the pill, under the weather, ordered to diet, or had trouble with your waterworks.
Patient:	I'm in the pink, doctor.
Doctor:	(**Exasperated**) Mr Watts, I have given you a full and thorough medical examination and found *nothing*. Temperature, pulse and blood pressure are normal. Reflexes are perfect. Eyesight and hearing are without fault. Balance is excellent. There is no sign of body malformation. Not even a blemish. According to the files, you have never had a day off work.
Patient:	No, doctor. I think that physical fitness is important.

Doctor:	(**Vengeful**) Do you smoke?
Patient:	No.
Doctor:	Fifty a day from now on. Do you drink?
Patient:	No.
Doctor:	I'm putting you on a hund ꞏd pints a week. I'm also prescribing late nights and regular sexual over-indulgence. And if that doesn't work, I'm sending you into hospital for observation. There's something seriously wrong with you, Mr Watts. You are abnormally healthy. We'll get to the bottom of this even if it kills you!

Would-be Professions

The calmest and most rational of human beings can become hot under the white collar about their professed status. However mundane their job, they will point to their appearance, qualifications and private language, and claim to belong to a profession by way of occupational therapy. If a suit is the distinguishing factor, be more respectful next time you bespeak to a bespoke tailor. If the passing of examinations is critical, every driving instructor can expect to be elevated to a higher rank. And if the use of a private and incomprehensible mumbo jumbo is to be taken seriously, then the Welsh constitute a profession!

This section allows five also-rans to canter along the course, though it could as easily be fifty. Everyone is after thoroughbred status. Of the five at present in the paddock all have been in the race for a long time. Advertising lives in the kingdom of cliché and has been trying to improve its brand image since it first began. Banking has built up its deposit account in the hopes of being able to afford professional recognition. Big business has openly tried to buy its way to respectability and set up Institutes and Management Courses with philanthropic zeal. Education puts the children first and its professional claims first and foremost. Selling is not just an arm of business but a large, fully-functioning, independent organ. Is it a job, an occupation, a vocation, or an affliction?

While not wishing to jump the gun, kick over the traces, or throw out the baby with the bathwater, this section thanks its lucky stars that all five would-be professions are tarred with the same brush. Each has a distinctive uniform. Each monitors the entry into its sacred ranks. Each has developed a special lingo that bonds it together at the same time as it keeps the outsider on the outside. Each offers careers rather than short-term jobs. Each has created its own impressive hierarchy. And each jealously guards its boundaries against raids from neighbouring occupations. Each is base metal that *would* be gold if it had the time.

To conclude this and the preceding section, an all-purpose professional letter has been added to meet all occasions and any emergency.

Advertising

Advertising is both its own worst enemy and best advertisement. It has created, adapted or otherwise immortalised the popular phrase. It has pioneered new slogans and rescued old adages from obscurity. With a tasteful blend of word and image, it has sold everything from tampons to television sets. It has Madison Avenued us into total submission. The cliché denizen of the jingle jungle is a shrewd, abrasive, calculating, coldly opportunist individual with expensive trendy clothes, unisex hair-styling and a determination to own a second Rolls Royce before the age of twenty-five. Vaulting ambition is channelled into the search for that elusive phrase that will set one product apart from its competitors. Beanz meanz Heinz and Advertising always anticipates Admass.

Advertisements for myself

Who am I?

Pleasing people the world over, the Holiday Inn guaranteed

to make me rise and shine from its Dunlopillo mattress and gaze out ('You only fit double-glazing once, so fit the best') at Everest.

I found a whole new experience in the bathroom, responded with zest, then thanked her with the gift of a Waverley pen because they, too, come as a boon and a blessing to men. Wearing the Colgate ring of confidence I set out to meet another day.

After the square meal nourishment of the sunshine breakfast, I succumbed to fresh cream cakes ('Naughty – but nice') and a refreshing cup of little perforations made in a Russell Hobbs kettle that was bubbling with bright ideas. When liquid engineering had thus fortified the over-forties, I realised it pays to decide Nationwide.

Confused by the choice between the ultimate driving experience, the little car that thinks big, the Japanese art of car-making, the new number to be reckoned with from Peugeot, the car that was better by design and the milestone in reliability, I remembered that this is the age of the train and went to work on a tin of Carnation milk because it is as versatile as an egg. On the journey I learned that happiness is a play called *Hamlet*.

For lunch I elected to call in at the local. Offered quality without compromise, the drink that goes down great with the sun, the beer that refreshes the parts other beers cannot reach, probably the best lager in the world, Skolarship, a born leader, a welcome awaiting, the uncommon spirit, quality in an age of change and French wine ('the affordable pleasure'), I fled from No Mann's Land pursued by a lotta bottles.

Because other pleasures pale beside it, I took to my bed with the first word in languages. It was distinctively longer and smoother and could take hot from cold and cold from hot. Though it lacked the patience of the listening bank at the sign of the black horse, it showed me how to clunk-click every trip with the mint with the hole. It combined the cookability of gas with the wonder of Woolworth's and taught me that it's a man's life in the Army and that small ones are more juicy, because everyone's a Cadbury's fruit and nut case if they eat Mr Kipling's exceedingly good cakes. Leaning across, I introduced myself.

I am John's left testicle. Gender advertising pays.

Banking

Banking is an occupational hazard. Whatever your walk of life, banking is on hand with a long leg to trip you up. It will pick you up somehow. Though not fully commensurate with the learned professions, it can pose as all three at once. It is the Law ('*That* is the verdict of this bank'): it impersonates the Church ('The Almighty will see you in his office'); and it offers Medicine ('Throw another bucket of water over him. I'll read out details of his overdraft more quietly next time'). The cliché denizen of the money maze is a middle-aged Minotaur who manages a local branch. Dressed in dark suits and dark expressions, he is protected by an invisible shield that wards off all excuses. Resentful and tardy in the extension of further credit, he is remarkably efficient in supplying data about what you owe him. Customers who have had enormous wins on the football pools and then sought his advice have actually seen him smile.

Cliché Jargon

Higher interest – if you'd care to raise your skirt a little more, Miss Phipps . . .

Overdraft facilities – a new cowl on the financial chimney.

Bank charges – robbery without violence.

Increased deposits – we've warned you about bringing that Black Horse in here!

Repayment tables – this week we sell the one in the kitchen, and next week it's the one in the dining room.

Cashpoint – the sharp end of banking.

Travel facilities – and if you book this policy you travel from solvency to bankruptcy in two fun-filled weeks.

Home improvement loan – borrowing enough money to evict your marital partner then barricade yourself in.

Teller – someone who won't tell you a thing.

Bank statement – No!

Liquid capital – I'm sorry, sir, but we cannot accept these fourteen thousand cases of Perrier water as collateral.

Cost breakdown – a bank customer in intensive care.

Banker's order – from now on, bounce all his bloody cheques!

Limited company – make it snappy. The manager can only allow you a two-minute interview.

Current account – one liable to sudden electrical discharge.

Big Business

Big Business moves in mysterious ways its wonders to perform. The cliché denizen of this dog-eat-dog world is the big, brash, balding, bellicose and unscrupulous boss of a multi-national corporation. This indefatigable and immaculately-dressed figure buys and sells in his sleep, hires and fires for exercise, and topples governments if the need arises. When he is not taking several simultaneous telephone calls in his inner sanctum on the fiftieth floor of a New York skyscraper, he is either making momentous decisions on a mid-Atlantic Concorde ('Ice, please, but no soda . . .') or giving his secretary lessons in shorthand on the fourposter in her penthouse flat in Mayfair. Whichever corner of the globe he is born in, the big businessman is always aggressively and disarmingly American.

Cliché Jargon

Memorandum of Association – lipstick on the collar.

Incentive Scheme – as from the New Year, the company intends to start paying its employees.

Rates of interest – the number of directors who doze off during a board meeting.

Brand manager – heat that iron up and have the ropes ready. The new intake of salaried staff will be arriving at any moment.

Market research – we want a door-to-door survey of the projected demand for our bodyline bras. Get busy on those knockers.

Budgetary control – feed him on Trill twice and day and be sure to change his water.

Double entry – please forgive me, Miss Withers. My aim has been affected by that fourth glass of brandy.

Preference shares – ones with the flavour you like best.

Meeting a claim – that is preposterous! I was at a Sales Conference in Karachi at the time when the alleged offence occurred.

Contract hire – eliminating competition by going into the removal business.

Profit margin – this year the Managing Director will be spending only three months on holiday in the Bahamas.

Sales resistance – has our representative had the bullet taken out yet?

Critical path analysis – order a new red carpet outside my office!

Personnel Department – a unit designed to recruit yes-men and yes-please-women.

Education

The teaching profession is an umbrella organisation for trade unionists. Cliché denizens of the blackboard jungle include the absent-minded Head who has difficulty remembering the names of his colleagues let alone those of the pupils; the tough, tight-lipped, tight-arsed, termagant Deputy Head with her spinster hair in a bun and her manifold energies dedicated to her role as the hired gun at the school; the young, sceptical, leftist and leather-jacketed English teacher who wants to put Brecht on every syllabus; and the bland, beaming, we-don't-want-to-rock-the-boat man from 'the Office' whose function is to control spending, suppress criticism, defend the status quo, act as a wet blanket on any fiery new educational ideas, and justify the ways of Sir Keith Joseph to man. Universities and polytechnics have their own cliché staff but it is on the school that we focus attention here. In education, it is the teachers who are taut.

Cliché Jargon

End-of-term report – a device used almost exclusively by cartoonists for evaluating the record of a particular government.

Morning assembly – two hymns, two prayers and a football result.

Extra-mural activities – boys relieving themselves against the walls of the school.

Mixed ability groups – bisexual orgies.

A late developer – I'm sorry, David, but at forty-six you simply must be viewed as a potential school-leaver.

The Great Debate – and the next question which this staff meeting must discuss is this: should we step up Lavatory Patrols or not?

Homework – something invariably done at school.

Careers advice – have you considered moving? There are much nicer parts of the country where you can be unemployed than here.

Public schools – private ones.

Approved schools – those for pupils who meet disapproval.

Night school – ones open in the evening and closed at night.

Single sex education – advanced masturbation classes.

Deschooling society – and if I find the boy who set fire to the Chemistry Laboratory . . .

P E Instructor – KGB – trained in torture techniques.

The School Trip – drug abuse behind the bike sheds.

Doors of opportunity – The *Times Educational Supplement*, an array of escape hatches that lead to other cells.

Selling

Professional salespersons have achieved amazing results in their chosen fields but does this make selling a profession? Is the ice cream vendor in the same mystic brotherhood as the seller of nuclear power stations? Can the Avon lady be compared with the marketing managers in aviation? The cliché denizen of Gift of the Gabland is a smooth, spivvy, plausible young man in a Burton suit and a permanent smile, trying to unload a second-hand car on a gullible customer. The act of selling is far more important than the item being sold and the tone of voice is at once urgent and reassuring. For salesmen everywhere life is simply a question of getting a foot in the door.

Cliché Jargon

The soft sell – there's such a tremendous demand for these hand-woven, top quality Indian carpets that you'd be doing me a favour by not buying this last one.

The hard sell – my bargain offer, exclusive to you and setting a precedent for generosity, is only open for one hour. Much as I hate to rush you into a decision, I recommend that you take advantage of this giveaway price some time in the next fifty-nine minutes . . .

Body language – I do beg your pardon! It was those faggots.

The killer instinct – buy the bloody thing or I'll shoot!

Visual aids – and with each interior spring mattress sold, we give this set of dirty postcards free.

A superior product – the one you are selling at any given moment.

An inferior product – the identical product sold last week.

Code of Practice – he who sells most laughs last.

Clinching the deal – put it this way, Mr Johnson, if *I* was buying an abbatoir myself then *this* is the one I'd plump for and no mistake!

Customer evaluation – if you'd just let me glance at the contents of your wallet, I think I may be able to save us both a great deal of time.

Business cards – the game is quite straightforward. The first person to be dealt a black queen has to buy this caravan.

Selling to the Top – what you really need is a Whip.

The Company Profile – and this is a photograph of the side elevation of our factory.

Controlling interviews – if you will just allow me to put this sticking plaster over your mouth, I can begin my sales patter.

Professional correspondence

The Old Rectory,
Pushard Maternity Hospital,
Inner Temple,
Department of Education,
The City.

December 25, 1983.

Our ref – VAT 69.
Your ref – Arthur Ellis.

Dear Sir or Madam,
   Thank you for your letter of the 14th inst. which is receiving attention in the new Science Laboratory. The goods the subject matter of your esteemed order have been sent to you by post/air/sea and appear to have been lost in transit. With the Church's blessing, we will send replacements without extra charge, investigate the situation and contact our carriers forthwith. An early settlement of this overdue account is therefore advised or we shall be obliged to put the whole matter in the hands of our Legal Department at the Stock Exchange.
   The sad news of your husband's/wife's passing was received at Head Office today, and on behalf of the Directors and Staff I tender our sympathies to you and the rest of the hospital ancillary workers in your loss. As some measure of tangible help at this time of trouble we seize this opportunity to recommend our standard all-weather casket in polished rosewood with brass handles. The bishop wishes it to be known that he intends to officiate in person at the funeral if he can locate his garden spade. In the meantime, we sincerely hope that you will enjoy full satisfaction with the Clerk of the Court.
   Though great care will be taken to ensure the Inspector's safety, the Headmaster is obliged to remind you that he cannot accept responsibility for any damage caused during the tour of the school. It has never been our policy to purchase HB pencils in such large quantities and we should therefore be grateful if you could send the twenty-seven pantechnicons to our premises in order to take delivery of the aforesaid consignment before the entire Advertising Agency expires from graphite poisoning. We remain at all times your humble servants should you wish to favour us with your instructions at some future date in the calendar.
   Despite an error in the computer print-out and staff shortages in the

wake of the seasonal holidays, your letter of resignation will be given sympathetic consideration and you will be accorded the benefit of regular visitors to the prison where you are at present residing. The disappearance of the firm's Cortina must be accounted for by you or we shall be left with no alternative but to order a replacement out of petty cash. To this end we have cancelled all engagements until further notice. We append herewith a schedule containing particulars of your defamatory remarks about hospital administration and beg leave to remind you that your other arm is in perfect working order.

This correspondence is now at an end. By the time that we resort to litigation, we sincerely trust that you will have learned a modicum of courtesy. Your share-value has sunk to a disagreeable low and we are forced to declare you a bankrupt.

With all good wishes,
Yours faithfully,

PS In conclusion, we extend the compliments of the season to you . . .

Theatre

The origin of theatre is lost in the mists of *Timon of Athens*. It was common practice among the Greeks between consenting adults in public. The Romans came, saw, re-cast and divided all Gaul into three acts with decent intervals. In short, long before a certain Jewish carpenter produced his first Miracle Play, theatre was a recognised phenomenon. It, too, had lived in Arcadia and heard the chimes at midnight of the three-minute bell.

Theatre is simple. Like lovemaking in a bored marriage, it consists of performer and spectator locked together in a shared experience. Exposition, development, dénouement and – Darling, you were wonderful! Time and space forbid a detailed examination of all the cliché categories of drama, but most of them have found a nesting-place in one particular play. Superstititon prevents the weak-minded from even mentioning the name of this versatile piece but we need not be deterred by its strange reputation. Let us list away.

The play is set in Scotland (Regional Theatre). It begins with thunder, lightning and three witches (Supernatural Drama). A fierce battle is being fought in the wings and a Bleeding Sergeant staggers on to give an eye-witness account (Realism). Meanwhile, on a blasted heath (Pastoral), three witches confront the soldier who plays the title-role (Military Drama) and tell him that he shall be king hereafter (Prophetic Theatre). At the palace Duncan, the king here and now, talks about the execution of the Thane of Cawdor (Thriller). Hot from the heath, our hero learns that he is to be the new Thane, thus fulfilling one of the witches' prophecies (Naturalism).

We move to an ancient castle (Historical Drama) where the wife of the new Thane reads out his letter and then in a single speech of iambic pentameters (Verse Drama) tells us what is going to happen in the rest of the play (Morality). After a

considered pause (Interlude) her husband arrives to learn that he must murder the king (Melodrama). Duncan, a symbol of kingship under grave threat (Expressionism), visits the castle because it hath a pleasant seat for the royal bum (Theatre in the Round). Little does he know (Mystery) that his host plans to stab him in his bed (Horror).

But the usurper has second thoughts (Stream of Consciousness). Enter his good lady who bullies him into evil (Slice of Life). The profane Thane does a solo turn with an invisible dagger (Dramatic Monologue) before going upstairs (Attic Comedy) to do the dirty deed offstage (Greek tragedy). His wife chides him about the bloody daggers, grabs them, ignores the pounding on the door, and races off (Knockabout Farce). Hubby hopes he can conceal his guilt (Masque).

A common porter (Prose Drama) who has been drinking (Pub Theatre) with the servantry (Kitchen Sink) takes an eternity (Pantomime) to open the door to Macduff and Lennox (Double Act). The murder is discovered and they over-react (Opera). Malcolm and Donalbain, sons to the king, are annoyed by the news (Angry Young Men) and flee. The villain becomes king and has Banquo killed by three murderers who inexplicably fail to finish off Banquo's son (Theatre of the Absurd).

Banquo's ghost haunts the new king (Miracle Play). Wifey sends the guests home and tries to calm her man down (Sit Com) Thunder brings in Hecate and the witches and a song is sung (Musical). There are still Two Acts to go (Epic Theatre). Soliloquies, sleep-walkers and perambulating trees tax the spectators' indulgence (Audience Participation), but they are rewarded with the sight of the severed head of the villain and an invitation to go to Scone (Well-Made Play).

This Dagger Saga is deservedly a classic in the Hall of Clichés. Let us banquet in the hall and count the other ghosts . . .

Classics

Classical drama created classic clichés. What scholars call the themes and conventions of Greek and Roman Theatre are really no more than a set of templates. Tragedy and comedy alike duplicated a pattern so carefully that performance had the quality of ritual. It was Aristotle, that self-appointed umpire, who drew up the official rule-book. Drama was to have six elements – Plot, Character, Thought, Diction, Music and Spectacle. Over two thousand years later, often without realising it, playwrights still page the Oracle of Greece.

Medieval drama, of course, was cliché from nativity to resurrection. Moralities and Tudor interludes were even more clockwork in design. Audiences did not watch them for novelty or surprise. The Golden Age of Elizabethan Drama brought a new set of stereotypes into play. Even Will Shakespeare, the best of the bunch, relied heavily on cliché characters in stock situations taken from standard plots. His genius lay in investing the familiar with a fresh significance. New lamps for old – but still lamps.

No dramatist before or since has supplied us with so many hackneyed quotations. As befits his finest play, *Hamlet* has by far the finest collection. Shakespeare turned succeeding generations into so many Polonius figures, endlessly mouthing the same phrases and advice. Even today the tragical-comical-historical-pastoral play survives. And Shakespeare himself has become the world's cliché playwright.

Restoration drama adjusted the rules somewhat and eighteenth-century playwrights were forced to make further alterations. Melodrama dominated the nineteenth century. Our own century has seen the rise and fall of the well-made play, the arrival and departure of the kitchen-sink drama, and the comings and goings of the Theatre of the Absurd. Each

174

new form is a development of an old cliché, each experiment flirts unwittingly with repetition.

Of all the arts drama is the one most haunted by the past. That strange noise in the wings is not the theatre ghost: it is dear old Aristotle still on the prompt-book.

Titles

Everyman
Hobson's Choice
A Mad World, My Masters
The Apple Cart
Much Ado about Nothing
Wild Oats
Dirty Linen
The Way of the World
You Never Can Tell
All's Well That Ends Well

Plots

A contest between Good and Evil in which the former always triumphs.

Murder and revenge in royal families.

Love stories with tragic consequences.

Love stories with happy endings.

Wars and lechery.

A savage indictment of the pillars of society or a compassionate look at the lower depths.

Biographical plays about important figures at key moments in history.

Assorted groups of people in an enclosed situation who can represent a microcosm of humanity under stress.

Class wars and sex wars.

A contest betwen Past and Present in which the former usually has the upper hand.

Characters

Everyman.

Assassinated heads of state, conspirators, usurpers, revengers and soliloquacious princes.

Star-crossed lovers in the mould of Romeo and Juliet.

Destined marital partners like Beatrice and Benedick.

Adulterous soldiers serving in plays that emphasise the futility of war.

People who talk interminably while they wait for Hamlet, Godot, Lefty, George and Margaret, death, rescue, a verdict, the felling of a cherry orchard or the final curtain.

Ghosts or figures from the past who haunt those living in the present.

Angry young men or middle-aged malcontents who rail against society in lengthy protest speeches that are strangely uninterrupted by others onstage.

Nascent feminists who assert themselves against husbands, lovers and employers and who indulge in symbolic actions such as murder, resignation, or the slamming of a door as they walk out of the house.

Absurd people with communication difficulties.

Dialogue

O! O! O!
Othello

O fie! fie! fie!
Measure for Measure

O horror! horror! horror!

Macbeth

Never, never, never, never, never.

King Lear

O day! O day! O day! O hateful day!

Romeo and Juliet

O what a rash and bloody deed is this!

Hamlet

O wonderful, wonderful and most wonderful Wonderful!

As You Like It

O, I am slain!
– I am maim'd for ever. Help ho, murder, murder, murder!

Othello

O madam, madam, madam!

Antony and Cleopatra

These words hereafter thy tormentors be!

Richard II Shakespeare

Is this the face that launched a thousand ships? And burnt the topless towers of Ilium?

Doctor Faustus Christopher Marlowe

I am Duchess of Malfi still.

The Duchess of Malfi John Webster

Much of a muchness.

The Provok'd Husband Sir John Vanbrugh

She's as headstrong as an allegory on the banks of the Nile.

The Rivals Richard Brinsley Sheridan

Arise, sir, from that semi-recumbent posture!

The Importance of Being Earnest Oscar Wilde

If only we could go back to Moscow! Sell the house, finish with our life here, and go back to Moscow.

Three Sisters Anton Chekhov

People don't do such things!

Hedda Gabler Henrik Ibsen

The strongest man in the world is the man who stands alone.

An Enemy of the People Henrik Ibsen

Mother, give me the sun.

Ghosts Henrik Ibsen

Put me into something loose.

The Gay Lord Quex Sir Arthur Wing Pinero

Stimulate the phagocytes.

The Doctor's Dilemma George Bernard Shaw

I am a Millionaire. That is my religion.

Major Barbara George Bernard Shaw

Walk? Not bloody likely! I'm going in a taxi.

Pygmalion George Bernard Shaw

Attention, attention must be paid to such a person.

Death of a Salesman Arthur Miller

We have to come back tomorrow.
  – What for?
  To wait for Godot.

Waiting for Godot Samuel Beckett

when, during wartime conditions many Mass Meetings fail to include, we shall remember something they may know nothing about.

Farce

Farce is fun. While other plays may set out to educate, edify, move, thrill, disturb, accuse, satirise or change the world, a farce simply entertains. It is the theatre of robust laughter and rolling in the aisles. Drama with its trousers down, letting it all hang out. Farce has a licence to flash.

The names are the first nudge – Lord Fancourt Babberley, Ada Hogg, Poppy Dickey, Fritzy Villiers, Brian Runnicles, Admiral Juddy, Gertrude Twine, Emma Hornett, Cyril Alcock, the Bishop of Lax, Reverend Lionel Toop, Reverend Oliver Purefroy, Reverend Cathcart Sloley-Jones, Gladys, Fred, Noony, Spettigue, Box, Cox and Carlos Homenides de Histuanga . . . Nobody would expect a gruelling tragedy or a piece of elevating social realism from this lot.

Funny names are matched by funny places full of funny objects. Characters are instantly recognisable types. There is no psychology, no interplay of emotion, no purpose, no message, no deeper chord of meaning. Plot rules and the rules of the plot demand continuous complications, embarrassments, mistaken identities, disguises and sudden reversals. The long arm of coincidence works overtime.

Clichés control the playing of farce as much as the writing of it. Funny walks, funny voices, funny clothes and funny make-up are part of the stock-in-trade of the farceur, who will also be an expert at goggle-eyed reactions, exaggerated gestures and dramatic double-takes. A mastery of comic business is essential so that the simplest of actions – pouring a drink, answering the telephone, sitting down – can become hilarious, especially when repeated time and again. The ability to race in and out of doors is a primary requisite.

Different countries set different boundaries for farce but its central territory is common to all. You know it at once by its time-honoured situations and its well-tried jokes. Farce must be fast, furious, frenetic, foolish and funny. Most of all, it must be familiar. When the trousers come down you know what you will see.

Titles

See How They Run
Tons of Money
Fringe Benefits
The Happiest Days of Your Life
Uproar in the House
Let Sleeping Wives Lie
Pillar to Post
Wild Goose Chase
Cuckoo in the Nest
What the Butler Saw

Plots

Long-lost twin brothers, whose servants are also twins, strive for a reunion.

Skeletons in the cupboard threaten a honeymoon and the husband labours frantically to keep them locked away from his wife.

Mishaps and mayhem in a haunted house.

Hilarious problems caused by unwanted corpses.

Two unfaithful husbands book in at the same hotel for a dirty weekend unaware that each is with the other man's wife.

A strange bequest – like being left five wives from a Sheik's harem – that upsets the calm and quiet of the ordinary English home.

Ex-prisoners arrive to dig up buried loot after years drooling about it, only to find that a house has been built over the spot where it is hidden.

An outwardly respectable man maintains two wives and families quite happily until the women become aware of each other's existence.

180

Familiar fun in the Army, Navy or Air Force when some raw recruits join up.

An administrative cock-up puts two schools, one male and one female, in the same building; or books two couples into the same bridal suite; or sells one house to two different buyers.

Characters

The errant husband.

The vengeful wife.

The monstrous ('I warned you not to marry him!') mother-in-law and the formidable ('Young man, what is the meaning of this?') father-in-law.

The fortune-hunter who never gets the fortune.

The man forced into disguise or drag in order to protect himself or maintain an illusion he has built.

The crafty manipulator or confidence trickster who takes advantage of the gullibility around him.

The likeable innocent who is always the main target for manipulators and misfortune.

Men or women with a comical ailment – deafness, gout, bad breath, a cleft palate and so on.

Funny vicars, policemen, politicians, servicemen, doctors, professors, servants, barmaids, publicans and gentlemen who lose their trousers.

People who eat, drink, smoke, laugh, steal, sleep, fuck, shout, hiccup or do anything else to excess.

Dialogue

Brazil. Where the nuts come from!

Charley's Aunt Brandon Thomas

I'm sure, Mr Box, you couldn't feel more if she had been your own intended.
— *If* she'd been *my own intended!* She *was* my own intended.

Box and Cox J M Morton

I could have pardoned everything but this last act of disobedience. You are unworthy of the Deanery. Leave it for some ordinary household.
— If I leave the Deanery, I shall give my reasons and then what'll folk think of you and me in our old age?
— You wouldn't spread this tale in St Marvells?
— Not if sober, sir — but suppose grief drove me to my cups?

Dandy Dick Pinero

What's your name?
— Death, sir . . .

Thark Ben Travers

Something written in the dust — GOS — Gossage.

The Happiest Days of Your Life John Dighton

Rookery Nook?
— Yes.
— Good. I'm coming here.

Rookery Nook Ben Travers

. . . that on the night in question you were nowhere near Wandsworth Common — that never in your life have you been on Wandsworth Common —
— But. Mr Price —
— that until this charge was brought against you, you had scarcely even *heard* of Wandsworth Common! *And*, on that night, far from being on Wandsworth Common, you were miles away in your home at — at — where *do* you live, by the way?
— Wandsworth Common.

Big . . . Bad . . . Mouse Philip King and Falkland Cary

A comic parson, eh? Well, you don't make me laugh. Your identification card.
— Certainly, Sergeant.

182

– Blimey! He's got one! 'Toop, Lionel, The Vicarage, Merton-cum-Middlewick.'

See How They Run Philip King

He said I looked like Boris Karloff!

Arsenic and Old Lace Joseph Kesselring

What weight you give it is a matter entirely for you.
   – Fifteen stone ten pounds.

One Way Pendulum N F Simpson

I said I am suing you for a hundred and fifty thousand dollars.
   – You mean – because you fell on our steps, Mr Whiteside?

The Man Who Came To Dinner George Kaufman and Moss Hart

I've never undressed in front of a man before.
   – I shall take account of your inexperience in these matters.

What the Butler Saw Joe Orton

Were you asleep?
   – Oh no!
   – Kiss me.
   – We can't.
   – Try. (*Their heads strain towards each other, fail to meet, fall apart again*)
   – Why this farce, day after day?

Endgame Samuel Beckett

. . . your wife has become increasingly suspicious of your all-night sittings.
   – She must know you were lying in more ways than one.
   – Blast you, Prendergast, blast my wife, and blast the lot of you! You don't seem to understand this lady and I had a very special relationship. She's a Member of Parliament as well.
   – Liberal, I suppose?

Uproar in the House Anthony Marriott and Alistair Foot

Melodrama

Melodrama is the most honest and least pretentious form of theatre. It is a drama of sensation for an audience which hungers after excitement and adventure. It is wish-fulfilment of the most obvious kind. Sentimentality on a spending spree. The cliché, the stereotype and the caricature are its basic elements and it glorifies them.

Some titles say it all in one word – *Drink, Pluck, Youth, Pleasure, Gin, Presumption, Remorse*. Others need to spread themselves – *The Night Porter, or the Dark Hearts of the Waterloo Road, Phantom in the Snow, or Wealth Not Happiness, Wild Will of the Ferry, or the Sailor and His Dog* (with the Destruction of the Murderer by the Fangs of the Faithful Dog!) Either way you're left in no doubt about what you are going to get. Drama with all the stops pulled out.

Black-and-white conflicts with vigorous action are the norm. They aim to thrill or to produce tears by their anguish. Chases, escapes, reprieves, rescues, shipwrecks, duels, hangings, drownings, explosions, fires and fights are standard practice. Heroic heroes, suffering heroines, sick children, wounded horses or dogs, heartless villains and drunken fathers hold season tickets for the two-hours' traffic of the stage. Virtue is rewarded, wickedness punished, loving hearts united, weaknesses reformed and dreams realised.

There is no place here to discuss the clichés of design and musical accompaniment that were used to reinforce the melodramatic effect; nor is there room to describe the cliché style of acting that was evolved with its repetitive vocal tricks, movements and gestures. Aiming at maximum identification with its audience, melodrama had everything worked out down to the last detail. Calculated culture.

It may offer little to the mind but it has copious delights for the eye and for the heart. It is crude, manipulative, over-written, corny, predictable, mediocre and shallow but it is also hugely entertaining and the repository of some of our finest clichés.

Titles

Destroyed by Drink
Saved from Crime
Taking the Veil
England's Glory
Time and Tide
Happiness at Home
It's Never Too Late to Mend
Love's Frailties
Pure as the Driven Snow
The Mother's Dying Child

Plots

Sensational murder.

Military heroism at a famous siege or battle.

Daring deeds at sea.

Gothic and Eastern Melodrama.

Last-minute escapes from impossible situations.

Cautionary tales about the demon drink.

People at the mercy of natural disasters such as flood, earthquake or avalanche.

Stories exemplifying the virtues of hearth and home.

Religion to the rescue in the darkest hour.

Domestic tragedies with obligatory death scenes.

Characters

The Hero. In or out of uniform.

The Heroine. In or out of distress.

The Villain. In or out of control.

The Old Man who bemoans evil days.

The Old Woman who recalls happy ones gone for ever.

The Child who is either a victim of a tragic situation or a tower of strength to his parents.

The Comic Man who provides low comic relief.

The Comic Woman who makes humour a double-act.

The Drunkard or Sinner who sees the error of his ways.

The Religious Symbol.

Dialogue

Georgina:	And you really feel sure that poor Mr Mordaunt has made me his heiress?
Sir John:	Ay, the richest heiress in England. Can you doubt it? Are you not his nearest relation? Niece by your poor mother, his own sister? All the time he was making this enormous fortune in India did we ever miss sending him reminiscences of our disinterested affection?
	Money Edward Bulwer-Lytton.
Susan:	Twelve long tedious months have passed, and no tidings of William. Shame upon the unkind hearts that parted us – that sent my

187

dear husband to dare the perils of the ocean, and made me a pining, miserable creature. Oh! the pangs, the dreadful pangs that tear the sailor's wife, as wakeful on her tear-wet pillow, she lists and trembles at the roaring sea.

Black-ey'd Susan Douglas Jerrold.

Brenno: Hold! You fly not! That passion burns in my veins, which, if you refuse to satisfy, force shall compel.

Innogen: Force!

Brenno: Think on your situation.

Innogen: Unhand me!

Brenno: You are alone.

Innogen: Monster!

Brenno: Your cries will be unheard.

Innogen: Oh, Heavens!

Brenno: Nay, this struggling –

Innogen: Help, help! Oh, Adelmorn!

Adelmorn: (*rushing from his concealment*) What shrieks! Villain, desist!

Adelmorn, The Outlaw Matthew Gregory Lewis

Gordon: Let me intreat your Grace to be more careful of your person, for poor old England's sake! (*he is shot dead at the termination of this speech*)

Duke: Heaven receive the faithful soldier! (*he is borne off*) Altho' I feel assured of winning this battle, from the steady bravery of my troops,

yet to win such a battle as gallant as this of
Waterloo at the expense of so many gallant
friends could only be esteemed a heavy
misfortune, were it not for its important
results to the public benefit. (*music – a horrible
discharge*)

The Battle of Waterloo J H Amherst

George: Oh! dear Uncle Tom! Do wake – do speak
once more! Look up! Here's Master George –
your own little Master George. Don't you
know me?

Tom: (*opening his eyes and speaking in a feeble tone*)
Mas'r George! Bless de Lord! it's all I wanted!
They haven't forgot me! It warms my soul; it
does my old heart good! Now, I shall die
content!

George: You shan't die! You mustn't die, nor think of
it. I have come to buy you and take you home.

Tom: Oh, Mas'r George, you're too late. The Lord
has bought me and is going to take me home.

George: Oh! don't die. It will kill me – it will break my
heart to think what you have suffered, poor
fellow!

Tom: Don't call me, poor fellow! I *have* been poor
fellow; but that's all past and gone now. I'm
right in the door, going into glory! Oh, Mas'r
George! *Heaven has come*! I've got the victory.
The Lord has given it to me! Glory be to his
name! (*Dies*)

(*Solemn music. George covers Uncle Tom with his
cloak and kneels over him. Clouds work on and
conceal them, and then work off*)

Uncle Tom's Cabin Harriet Beecher Stowe

Vivien:	I'm to be driven from the house like a dog. But he shall pay for it. (*takes glass from Mostyn*). He has spurned my love, but he forgets there is one thing left to me. (*drains tumbler*).
Mostyn:	What's that?
Vivien:	Revenge! (*hurls glass with a crash into fireplace – fire blazes as brandy pours on it. Curtain.*)

The Derby Winner Harris, Hamilton & Raleigh

Mathias:	(*alone – comes forward and listens with terror. Music with frequent chords*) Bells! Bells! (*he runs to the window and, slightly drawing the curtains, looks out*). No one on the road. (*comes forward*); What is this jangling in my ears? What is to-night? Ah, it is the very night – the very hour! (*clock strikes ten*) I feel a darkness coming over me. (*stage darkens*) A sensation of giddiness seizes me. (*he staggers to the chair*). Shall I call for help? No, no, Mathias. Have courage! The Jew is dead!

The Bells Leopold Lewis

Musicals

The musical is a chorus line of curvaceous clichés. They dance on our willing suspension of disbelief so that we do not count the leg-kicks; they pirouette through dialogue, lyrics, orchestration, set, costumes, lighting and, of course, choreography. In no form of theatre does the stereotype have quite so many curtain calls. But let the musical defend itself. It is entitled to sing its own song.

Ain't there anyone here for love? All I need is a girl. Could it be you? Do I hear a waltz? Do I love you? What kind of fool am I? Bess, you is my woman. Flash! Bang! Wallop! Well, did you ever . . .?

I ain't down yet. I'm going to like it here. I can't sit down, I can't say no, I couldn't sleep a wink last night. I feel pretty, I love Paris, I enjoy being a girl. If I ruled the world, if I were a bell, if I were a rich man, if my friends could see me now, if this isn't love then I'm gonna wash that man right outa my hair and leave my heart at the stage door canteen in an English garden.

Don't let it bother you. I got it bad (and that ain't good) but I got rhythm, I got the sun in the morning, I'm all smiles, I'm a brass band, I'm an Indian, too, I'm on my way, I'm the greatest star, I'm just wild about Harry and I still see Elisa – in our little den of iniquity. I could write a book!

You are beautiful – you and the night and the music. You do something to me. You are a woman, I am a man. You have cast your shadow on the sea. You'd be so nice to come home to. You're the cream in my coffee, you're always in my arms, you're the top. Young and foolish, sweet and lowdown, fine and dandy, you'll never get away from me and you've got to pick a pocket or two.

I believe in Bill, Camelot, heather on the hill, Hernando's hideaway, Kansas City, night and day, Pedro the fisherman, promises, rain in Spain, serenade, sunrise, sunset, wand'rin' stars, soft lights and sweet music. With a song in my heart, I can give you the starlight.

The cliché has found its niché.

Titles

Face the Music
And so to Bed
Out of this World
When in Rome
Wish You Were Here
Crest of the Wave
Anything Goes
Best Foot Forward
On the Town
Salad Days

Plots

Oppressed family sings its way to freedom.

Let's-put-on-a-musical-in-a-barn.

Shipboard romance or water-based drama.

Modernised and musicalised classics.

Stories which illustrate the power of love to join the most unlikely couples – Cossack officer and singer, confidence trickster and librarian, matchmaker and parsimonious storekeeper.

An evocation of a vanished world deemed to be fascinating and characterful – British Music Hall, America in the Twenties, France in Lautrec's day.

Rock musicals that translate the Bible into contemporary terms.

Biographies of showbiz personalities such as singers, film stars, strippers, impressarios or composers.

The little man coming up hard against the big world but surviving

192

thanks to his basic commonsense, the love of a good woman, and a firm grasp on all the best songs in the show.

Satirical musical that attacks war, big business, government, the ethics of commercial theatre or some other familiar target.

Characters

Happy heroes or tormented anti-heroes. Singing Shakespearean types.

Innocent girls educated by experience.

Nightclub singers and whores.

Base villains with base voices who meet death, arrest, or redemption through the magic of music.

Wry old folks who impart advice to headstrong youngsters and who are always proved right.

Rootin', tootin', tough-as-they-come tomboys who are gradually softened by romance.

Fresh-faced young men with a talent for being best friends, providing comic relief, and soldiering on through the subordinate love interest.

Confidence tricksters, salesmen, preachers, circus performers, fairground barkers and other extroverts.

A chorus of singing nuns, children, soldiers, sailors, farmers, cowmen, Jets, Sharks, pierrots, gypsies, prisoners, street urchins, rock Christians, vagabonds, Can Can dancers, secretaries, hoodlums, visitors to Ascot, wedding guests, German students, professional entertainers, colourful Cockneys, peasants, Mounties, lords and ladies at the Court of King Arthur, workers, strikers and darkies.

Dialogue

They ain't nobody goin' to slug out anythin'. This here's a party! Sing it, Andrew!

Oklahoma

194

Lucentio, thou meacock wretch!
I hate men . . .

Kiss Me Kate

I didn't believe hard enough.
  – Loving is enough.
  – They won't let us be.
  – Then we'll get away.
  – Yes, we can. We will.
Hold my hand and we're halfway there . . .

West Side Story

Why do people have to lose things to find out what they mean?
  – Take a last look and let's start walking. I got lost around here once.
Brigadoon, Brigadoon . .

Brigadoon

Look, pa! Gold! Gold!
  – So anyhow, here's Jim, Lord. I hope you'll make him happy up there . . . for-ever-and-ever-I-stake-this-claim-Amen!

Paint Your Wagon

Everything you had in Glocca – and more. Do you hear that skylark?
  – Aye!
  – The same as in Ireland.
  – Aye, a Glocca Morra skylark.

Finian's Rainbow

Women of England – do your duty. Send a man to enlist today.
  – Have you an able-bodied groom, chauffeur or gamekeeper serving you?
  – If so, shouldn't they be serving their country?

Oh What a Lovely War

My only fear is that suddenly I shall wake up. **This is my lovely day . . .**

Bless the Bride

Meine Damen und Herren, Mesdames et Messieurs, Ladies and Gentlemen . . . Comment ça va? Do you feel good?

Cabaret

Oh, Macheath! Was it for this we parted? Taken! Imprisoned! Tried! Hanged! Cruel reflection! I'll stay with thee till death – no force shall tear thy dear wife from thee now. What means my love? – not one kind word! Not one kind look! Think what thy Polly suffers to see thee in this condition. **Thus when the swallow seeking prey . . .**

The Beggar's Opera

Damn Mrs Pearce, and damn the coffee, and damn you!

My Fair Lady

He's as poor as a synagogue mouse.

Fiddler on the Roof

No. Ye see, I dinna want to jus' get married. I think ye should only do it when ye and your lad want to stay together fiercely an' gettin' married is the only way ye can do it that's proper.
  – That's an unusual idea, Fiona.

Brigadoon

A rescue! A rescue! I was sure of it. Where the need is greatest, there will God's help be nearest.
  – A rescue! A rescue! My dearest Mackie has been rescued. I am so happy.
  – So, now the whole thing has a happy end!

The Threepenny Opera

Pantomime

I am the King of Clichés
In the Land of All The Same,
Twankeys and Washee Wishées
Know that Panto is my name.

I'm fairytale and romance,
Nursery rhyme and show,
Music, farce and tap dance,
And jokes from long ago.

I entertain the nation
As cow or cat or clown,
I'm audience participation
When I pull my song sheet down.

You all adore my bawdy,
My thrills and laughs and sighs,
My costumes, bright and gaudy,
My girls with sexy thighs.

You like my Cinderellas
To dance in marble halls
With Sisters who are fellas
And never miss their Balls.

I'm corn, I'm old potato,
I'm best traditional ham.
Modernise? I'd hate to –
You love me as I am!

Now for my Grand Finale!
Thank you all for coming here
With the kids and Uncle Charlie.
Merry Christmas and Happy New Year!

Titles

Aladdin
Babes in the Wood
Cinderella
Dick Whittington
Jack and the Beanstalk
Little Red Riding Hood
Mother Goose
Robinson Crusoe
The Sleeping Beauty
Humpty Dumpty

Plots

Comical capers in colourful China involving boy with a magic lamp and a wicked uncle.

Forest frolics involving children left alone in a wood but protected by various animals and by Robin Hood and his Merry Men.

Rollicking romance involving a young girl who is kept as a household drudge by her Ugly Sisters, but who goes to the Ball with the aid of her Fairy Godmother, and ends up marrying the Prince.

Medieval mirth involving a young man who sets out for London with little more than a talking cat and who finishes up as Lord Mayor of the city.

Gargantuan giggles involving a boy who climbs a huge beanstalk, discovers a castle, is at the mercy of the giant who lives there, escapes and returns home richer and wiser.

Woodland whimsy involving a young girl in red whose visit to her grandmother takes on a strange turn when the old lady is swallowed by a Big Bad Wolf, who then tries vulpine villainy on the girl.

Feathery fun involving a poor old woman on the point of eviction who becomes rich when her goose begins to lay golden eggs, but who lets her wealth go to her head until she is chastened by experience.

Marooned merriment involving a sailor cast ashore on a desert island that is inhabited by singers, dancers, pirates, unwanted relatives and all manner of flotsam.

Heart-rending hilarity involving a princess who is the victim of a spell that makes her fall into a deep sleep, but who is eventually awakened by the kiss of a handsome prince.

Eggy exhilaration involving a rotund hero, a wall, a fall, all the king's horses and all the king's men.

Characters

The Dame.

The Principal Boy.

The Principal Girl.

Buttons and other Best Friends.

The Villain or Wicked Fairy.

The Good Fairy.

The Comic Duo.

The Speciality Act.

Dancers.

Animals.

Dialogue

Welcome, my friends! Come spend a happy time,
Enjoy once more the world of Pantomime!

New lamps for old, new lamps for old!

I fight the wicked and help the good!
My name, by the way, is Robin Hood!

You *shall* go to the Ball, Cinders!

Turn again, Whittington,
Turn again to London!

Hey, Dandini!

Fee-fi-fo-fum,
I smell the blood of an Englishman.
Be he alive, or be he dead,
I'll grind his bones to make my bread.

Grandmamma, what great ears you have!
   – All the better to hear you with my dear.
   – Grandmamma, what great eyes you have!
   – All the better to see you with, my dear.
   – Grandmamma, what great teeth you have!
   – All the better to eat you with, my dear.

Look, Mother Goose! In the Pool of Eternal Youth!
There's a shark's fin!
   – Probably my agent.

Well, m'lads, today I shall sail away with my brother, Captain
Robinson Crusoe, to have a peep at some Foreign Parts . . .

In that castle is a princess, the most beautiful ever seen; and
she must sleep there one hundred years before she is
awakened by a king's son whom she is destined to marry.

We welcome you, Queen Spritely,
We welcome you politely
By bowing very, very low,
In manner truly knightly.

Wishee Washee, will you wash my washing nice and bright?

Meee-ow, ow, ow, ow, ow, ow, ow!
— Bless my soul! A talking cat!

Priscilla, there you are!
— Quack! Quack!

Oh, no, there isn't!
— Oh, yes, there is!

Ah, Simple Simon, will you look after this old cow for me?
— Your mother can take care of herself.

Thrillers

Murder, though it have no tongue, will speak with most miraculous typewriter and it continues to provide most of the dialogue for thrillers. Rape, blackmail, embezzlement, treason, armed robbery and other crimes have their say but murder out-shouts them all. In commercial terms, it has consistently made a killing. Blood banks.

Murder has many forms. It can be committed, feared, suspected, feigned, threatened or theorised about. It may be horrific, amusing, brutal, accidental, inconvenient or well-deserved. Among its agents are men, women, children, animals and ghosts; among its victims are husbands, wives, hated employers, loved public figures and burdensome relatives with large fortunes to leave. Its favourite haunt is a box set. Its weapons are legion.

The whodunnit asks who did it but there are variations. Has a murder really been committed? Who will kill whom before the final curtain? Is the person on trial guilty or not guilty? Does the rich old lady realise that she is confiding in the very people who are planning to strangle her? How will the vengeful ex-mistress actually do it? Now that he has poisoned his wife and concealed her body in the linen cupboard, how will he get her out of a house that is full of guests? Afraid to do the deadly deed herself, whom can she hire and on what terms? Are the three victims really the work of the same murderer? Is the threatening letter a hoax? Can a mother be proved to be innocent of the crime sixteen years after she was supposed to have committed it? Is the perfect murder possible?

Thrillers are interrogatory. Question marks punctuate them and their sub-text is rich with alternative possibilities. Puzzle value must be high and there must be stomach-tightening suspense. It is mandatory that people are not what they seem. Any location may be used – country houses, railway stations, flats in Chelsea, Arctic explorers' huts – but the guessing game must be played.

Murder must tell its tale yet again. For a thriller to be worthy of its name, it must use a dead body to bait its mousetrap.

Titles

Sleuth
A Clean Kill
Dead on Nine
Guilty Party
Something to Hide
The Proof of the Poison
Suspect
Murder for the Asking
Wait Until Dark
Witness for the Prosecution

Plots

Conventional houseparty murder at Cheesecake Manor.

Conventional whodunnit disguised by a shift to an unusual location such as a convent, a lighthouse or a women's prison.

Tense courtroom drama in which the villain is only nailed (or the innocent person cleared) by a startling new piece of evidence at the eleventh hour.

Hostage dramas involving the intrusion into ordinary lives of danger, terror and casual death.

People are trapped in a remote farmhouse or other favourite location with an unknown killer in their midst or with a figure of menace coming to get them.

Complications arise when a husband or wife hires someone to kill their marital partner and it is the murderer who becomes the unintended victim.

The perfect murder, often committed by the man who is in charge of investigations and who is, as such, above suspicion.

Psychological thriller in which there is a conspiracy to persuade a central character that he or she is mad.

Supernatural happenings disturb a group of people in a location from which they cannot escape until the end of the play.

The whodunnit in which the burden of interest is on why-did-he-do-it or will-she-get-away-with-it?

Characters

Writers, artists, actors and media people.

Dogged detectives who get there in the end.

Victims who become aware of the plot against them and who turn the tables on would-be killers.

Brilliant barristers with histrionic skills.

Neighbours, servants, vicars, colonels, postmen, window cleaners and others hauled in to provide a vital clue as well as comic relief.

Murderers at a houseparty who can be identified at once because they are least likely to have done it and have the weakest apparent motive.

Red herring characters who lure suspicion onto themselves and whose eccentric behaviour turns out to have a simple explanation.

Mistresses, ex-mistresses, lovers and ex-lovers who blithely commit a crime of passion or who seek revenge.

People with a serious physical defect – blindness, paralysis, broken limbs – who so contrive things in the last act that they meet their persecutors on equal terms and defeat them.

Dead bodies.

205

Dialogue

Stay over there, all of you. Come over here, Anne, we'll give them a run for their money.
— Give me that gun, Redding.
— Don't come any nearer, Vicar.
— Give me that gun.
— You're being very foolish. One corpse more or less won't make any difference to me, you know.

Murder at the Vicarage Agatha Christie (dramatised by Moie Charles and Barbara Toy).

You'd better be going home, Mr Quincey.
— Home . . . They say murder will out! Murder will out! But not my murder! Not Harry Quincey's murder! My God! That's a good one.

Uncle Harry Thomas Job

You know, I never use the twelve-bore these days, except for the pigeons

Mr Fothergill's Murder Peter O'Donnell

Where's your brain, Fred? Just because a key is found on the *inside* of an unlocked door . . .
— Good Lord; you mean it could have been unlocked from the outside and the key slipped round in the general excitement of finding the body? Here, I'm a fool.
— Correct. Your first suggestion, I mean. And the third reason I don't believe it's suicide is the watch. Did you notice it? Before it was taken off?
— I saw he'd broken it on the chair as he fell.
— Never mind that. I mean that it's unusual for a man to wear his wrist-watch with the figure six at the top. Or, as we say in the force, upside down.
— Then it was put on *after* he was dead?
— Yes, and it's even more unusual he'd do that himself.
— Then it's murder . . .

Ten-Minute Alibi Anthony Armstrong

Oh, my darling.

206

– Tony, Tony, Tony.

– It's all right now. It's all right. What happened?

– He got something round my throat – it felt like a stocking . . .

– Let me see. (*He touches her throat gently and she turns her head away quickly*) Hurt? I'd better call a doctor.

– But isn't . . . isn't he dead?

– It's you that needs a doctor.

– No, I'm all right – but – is he . . .?

– Yes – he must have died instantly. There's hardly any blood. Must have driven those scissors right through himself.

– Horrible! Can't you . . . cover it up?

Dial M for Murder Frederick Knott

You – you didn't really do it? You didn't kill him?

– Of course I killed him! It was too good to be missed. I was doing him a favour – he *asked* me to do it. He *wanted* me to do it!

– Oh, no – no, Henry – you couldn't have – you couldn't have –

– It's all over, Dora, I told you – we're in the clear. The sergeant's satisfied. We're free and in the clear.

– But he thinks Mrs Franklyn did it!

– What of it?

– But she didn't!

Murder for the Asking Derek Benfield

Is this a trap? What's she been saying to you?

– Nothing at all. It's not hard to guess.

– Guess? Guess what?

– That you and your crook husband were getting money out of her.

– Don't talk like that about the dead . . .

No Escape Rhys Davies

Television

The origin of television is lost in the mists of time signals. For twenty-four hours a day it is involved in a game of Beat The Clock. Like Cinderella, it has heard the chimes at midnight. Like Mercutio, it knows when the bawdy hand of the dial is upon the prick of noon. Like ITN newcasters, it has learned to get in quickly between the Boings of Big Ben. Old Father Time is the Jaws in the haunted fishtank. Just when you thought it was safe to watch a programme again, he snaps it in half with a razor-toothed commercial break. It is the first cliché of the small screen that everything is cut down to size. The box only likes boxes of specific dimensions. All the news that fits.

Novelty and imagination are at a premium. They are on the Wanted posters of every television company. Huge rewards are offered for their capture, dead or alive. Once delivered by the bounty-hunters, they are kept under lock and key so that they cannot disturb the peace of the programmers. It is the stereotype that wears the tin badge. In a shoot-out with true originality he always has the fastest draw. Redskin ideas bite the dust.

The one-eyed monster in our living rooms has produced enough clichés to fill a hundred books. Here, however, we have had to be highly selective. Whole categories have had to be omitted and a few words are perhaps in order on each one. It is in the nature of a toast to absent friends.

News

With its rigid presentation this is essentially a form of light entertainment, since its main function is to provide an easy target for satirists, humorists and others who wish to bounce for fun on the common trampoline.

Current Affairs

Television's continuing Fancy Dress Ball. There is only one current affairs programme and it wears a thousand disguises. They change its title, its presenters, its cutting edge, its theme music but they cannot change its raison d'être. Current affairs simply discusses itself.

Religion

This is the ghost in the machine, the clammy hand on the shoulder of the viewer. Official reports deny that it exists at all, but strange cries come from the crypt on Sundays and shadowy figures flit across rood screens. Television companies would love to exorcise it but, for the moment, to mix a metaphor, religion is a cross they all have to bear.

Documentaries

Programmes in which some aspect of the human condition is tracked down, caught, caged, and subjected to painful examination by a point of view. Wounded for life, it is then released so that the crew can go on safari again for fresh game.

Children's Television

A reductive exercise in which adults pretend they are children and in which the younger generation apes its seniors. Children's television also serves as a dumping-ground for the dramatised novels of Dickens, Jane Austen, Defoe, Swift, the Brontës, Thackeray and other authors who wrote specifically for grown-ups.

Education

Loft insulation. A cheap and effective way of filling in that upper area in the house of television that is rarely visited in normal viewing hours.

Breakfast Television

Something that does not go snap, crackle and pop but just lies there soggy in the plate. For those who like to start their day with darkness.

Even if we exclude these bottomless pits of popular phrases, television still remains an Aladdin's Cave of sparkling clichés. We gain entry to the magic cavern and feast our eyes on:

Comedy 'Some mothers do 'ave 'em!'

212

Drama 'Pug Henry was one of the best naval officers in the US armed forces.'

Light Entertainment 'So it's good night from me – and it's good night from him.'

Sport 'This is the big one! He has it all to do! But – oh! – he's hit the woodwork again!'

It's an ill wind of war that blows nobody any good. Switch on, sit back and enter a world that is By The Finest Swordsman In All France Divided.

Comedy

A woman marries a man sixteen years younger than she is. An avowed racialist finds himself living next door to a black family. A rebel without a cause keeps shouting 'Power to the People!' A schoolteacher who wins the pools is killed by a champagne cork while celebrating and goes to heaven. A seedy old reprobate parks himself on his son and his daughter-in-law like an army of occupation. A randy middle-aged wife is mated with an impotent husband. Three pensioners pass the time of day by causing mischief in a Yorkshire village. A fast-talking American Army sergeant effectively runs the whole post. A new home-owner meets every problem in the book. A young man is an inveterate liar.

Situation comedy is like sex. There is a limit to the number of positions and some are vastly more comfortable than others. Depending upon your individual taste satisfaction can be achieved with twosomes, threesomes, foursomes or larger groups. Consummate success is unknown and the failure rate is embarrassingly high. The worst thing you can do is to try too hard.

Because the comedy series is the quickest way to raise a laugh among the ratings, it is a standard issue in most television companies. On paper it is relatively easy to create another winner. You hire proven comic talent from that select band of writers (like policemen, they usually work in pairs). You find a director with a sense of humour. And then you dip into that small pool of performers to fish out the big names. No comedy series is complete without Penelope Keith, Peter

Bowles, Ronnie Barker, John Alderton, Brian Murphy and Wendy Craig. If room can be found for Leonard Rossiter and Paul Eddington, all the better. Felicity Kendal, Richard Briers and Patrick Cargill are additional bonuses. These artistes and their American counterparts are skilled practitioners in disguising old situations with new perspectives, in lifting the viewing figures by raising an eyebrow and in setting an audience alight with a slow burn.

As far as the eye can see, it is Cliché Country. The characters are familiar, their predicaments are well-rehearsed, their dialogue has that hand-me-down quality to it and their comic routines have been common property from time immemorial. Laughter with old friends is the best kind there is. That is the situation that the comedy series exploits.

Titles

The Good Life
Nearest and Dearest
Tom, Dick and Harriet
Love Thy Neighbour
To the Manor Born
Till Death Us Do Part
Young at Heart
Life Begins at Forty
Open All Hours
Mind Your Language
Sweet Sixteen
In Loving Memory

Situations

Keeping up with the Joneses.

The British class system.

The Law, the Church, the Medical Profession.

Sworn enemies who are married, working together, or living next door to each other.

214

Men in prison or the armed services.

Occupational hilarity in teaching, taxi-driving, undertaking, building, writing, Agony-Aunting or working in a pub, a shop, a department store, a holiday camp, a repertory theatre, an office, the rag trade, on the buses or in the rag and bone business.

Wartime nostalgia featuring land girls, POW's, comical Krauts, bungling British officers, the black market, the Home Guard and evacuees.

A family in which each individual member hates all the others. Communal misunderstandings.

Sexual urges constantly thwarted.

People facing slightly unusual situations such as having a baby in middle age, moving to the country from the town, running a private hotel that is more like a lunatic asylum or sharing accommodation in an unconventional way.

Divorcees who tiptoe towards remarriage to each other, though neither is prepared to admit that this is what they really want.

Characters

The complete fool.

The hen-pecked husband or the long-suffering wife.

Teenage children who are a continuous problem.

Irascible or doddery old folk who live-in, arrive without warning, or otherwise upset a young couple's domestic bliss.

Funny families who operate as a unit in the mould of The Dukes of Hazzard, The Beverley Hillbillies *or* The Addams Family.

The comic duo – father and son, mother and daughter, flat mates, likely lads, boss and secretary, employer and valet, husband and wife, and so on.

Wildly differing characters who work together and unite against a common enemy in the shape of a loathed superior.

The Best Friend, who is identical in all but name and appearance to the Hero or Heroine, and whose function is to act as a sounding-board for him or her.

Lovers whose path to marriage, cohabitation or happiness is strewn with insurmountable obstacles.

Loners, little men, single girls and rebels against society.

Silly asses and pompous bosses.

Funny foreigners.

Female battleaxes.

Comical clergymen, judges, doctors, politicians, civil servants and other pillars of society.

Dialogue

Oo, Bettee! The pussy's done a whoopsy in the caravan!

It ain't half hot, mum.

Are you free, Mr Humphries?

Please, sir . . .

Manuel, you're a complete and utter nincompoop! – Si.

Permission to step out of line, Captain Mainwaring?

Hello, campers ! Rise and shine!
    – Can I be a yellowcoat?

Harold! Harold!
    – You dirty old man!

Now let's not do anything rash.
  – It's against union rules! Everybody out!

You are in the realms of fantasy, Compo.
  – Yeah, thinkin' about Nora Batty's stockin's!

The Labour Bloody Party is to blame! That's right, innit! I mean, innit! Don't you know nuffin', you silly moo!

Yes, Minister . . . No, Minister . . . Of course, Minister.

Hey, Fletch, do us a favour, will you?
  – Naff off!

I suppose one might say that all's well that ends well.
  – Very apt, sir.
  – All the same, your methods were a trifle rough, what?
  – One cannot make an omelette without breaking eggs, sir.
  – Right ho, Jeeves . . .

I didn't like it at all, Mildred. It was a big disappointment.
– That's the story of my life, George!

You say that? To a man of my calibre? I call that a diabolical liberty, mate!

Does it hurt?
  – Only when I laugh.

Who's the gaffer around here?

Get your haircut, lovely boy!

I'm sorry, father. Am I interrupting you?
  – No, darling, I was only trying to write a book. Feel free to barge in here and stop my gainful employment at any time.

Oh, Brother!

Drama

Drama is the brightest jewel in television's crown though most of it is imitation. Even with the one-shot play – ostensibly the drama of free expression – the tendency is towards the cliché and the formula. Vogue is a determining factor as is a fixed time-slot, and limitations of budget can wipe the smile off the most imaginative drama. The habit of grouping plays under titles such as *Love Story* or *Play For Today* imposes further restrictions by denoting subject-matter or controlling attitude.

Our concern here is with drama series and serials, the areas in which the formula technique runs riot. The series is a succession of self-contained episodes featuring regular characters while the serial is a continuous narrative that has been chopped up into set lengths and linked together by cliffhangers. Both obey the same rules, but the relentlessness of the serial calls for a higher level of incident and a more frequent and unashamed descent into melodrama. The greatest accolade that can be bestowed on a series or serial is to say that it is interchangeable with another of its breed. Only then has it arrived at total cliché control.

Titles fall into three main groups. Names win all hands down – *Kojak, Quincy, Barlow, Cannon, Maverick, Maigret, Bergerac, Callan, McCloud, Columbo, Mackenzie, Hadleigh, Adam Adamant, Sam, Clare, Juliet Bravo, Fox, Cribb, Hazel, Dr Kildare, Sergeant Cork, Starsky and Hutch, Cagney and Lacey, Hardcastle and McCormick*, to mention but three. Functions figure largely – *Doomwatch, Special Branch, Minder, Task Force, The Plane Makers, Probation Officer, Riviera Police, Headmaster, Rifleman, The Samaritans, Spycatcher* and so on and so forth. Places are ever-popular. You can visit *Crossroads, Weavers Green, Coronation Street, Flamingo Road, Peyton Place, General Hospital, Harpers West One, Dallas, Knots Landing, Brookside, The Crezz, Hill Street Blues, Frontier, Swizzlewick, County Hall*, or, for the second time, *Brideshead*.

Over fifty programmes have been mentioned here but they fit into a very small number of categories. Repetition is the keynote. Series and serials strive to build up a steady alliance with an audience by offering them a reassuring sameness. Within their rigidly prescribed limits, writers and directors attempt to ring the changes but they are all pulling on identical bells. It really is a case of drama for old rope. At its most definitive, the television series and serial is shot in clichérama.

Television Drama Series

Titles

Justice
Within These Walls
Flesh and Blood
On the Line
The Main Chance
Softly, Softly
We'll Meet Again
Public Eye
Upstairs, Downstairs
The Spoils of War

Storylines

Cops and robbers.

The Wild West.

I Spy.

Hospital drama.

Wartime nostalgia.

A fabulously rich family undergoes an interminable succession of crises in the bedroom, boardroom, courtroom and political arena.

Women trapped – in gaol, in a convent, in a girl's boarding school, in a marriage, in a man's world, in a POW Camp somewhere in the Far East.

Historical hokum set in the time of the Plantagenets, the Tudors, the Civil War (English or American), the French Revolution or the nineteenth century.

Pseudo-biographies of the randier royals and the most scandalous statesmen of the past.

Taking the lid off the working world of a particular group of people such as policemen, probation officers, nurses, barristers, local councillors, journalists, industrialists, spies, scientists, servicemen and brave sheriffs of lawless towns.

Characters

The private investigator who wages a personal war against the crime wave and who contrives to be in the right place at the right time despite regular death threats.

Gimlet-eyed spycatchers who smoke out moles.

The beautiful young woman who inherits wealth, position or a dramatic situation and who then confounds all those around her by the forceful way in which she responds.

Ruthless businessmen who stop at nothing as they play their desperate power games and toy with politicians and voluptuous mistresses.

The handsome new doctor who is haunted by a secret sorrow, tormented by the memory of a patient whose life he believes he could have saved, and who is therefore ripe for a romantic entanglement of the most serious kind.

Loners, oddballs, idealists, mavericks, misfits, troublemakers and outsiders who toss a spanner into the works at every available opportunity.

Peace-loving and law-abiding cowboys with rugged profiles and nice smiles who are forced to take up a gun to protect someone or something.

Cardboard captains of spaceships or leaders of lunar communities who are programmed to evince all the acceptable virtues, and who chart a course through the most mind-boggling danger without batting an eyelid.

The policemen, crooks, cowboys, spies, business colleagues or friends who can only function as a twosome and who adopt the characteristics of the cliché double-act.

Comic servants and colourful low-lifers in historical costume who are always burdened with period slang and who give us another perspective on those of higher social rank.

Dialogue

Aye, Ned, lad. Where there's muck, there's brass.

Who loves ya, baby?

Evening, all!

Get your horses! We'll head 'em off at the pass!

Beam us up, Scotty.

Take my advice, Major, and forget all thought of escape. You are in Colditz now and you are here to stay.

Simon Templar! I might have known!

We're very poor, Mr Petrocelli. We can't pay you much.
 – Don't worry about the dough. This one's on me.

Go on. Gizza job, gizza job, go on. I could do that.

Bodie? Doyle here. He's got the girl. Put a tail on him!

Do my eyeballs deceive me, Terence?

No Lacey ever died better. I think he would not have wished to live beyond this day.

Well, as my ole grandpappy used to say to me . . .

Bad news, guv. Heard it on the grapevine. He's out.

Go to the master of this castle and tell him that Geoffrey Plantagenet and his son, the Duke of Normandy, will spend the night here.

I'm warning you, Reilly. This is your last chance.

Ben Casey is the finest doctor is the whole state.

Why, heck, Sue Ellen! Now you don't *mean* all those nasty things you're saying about JR, do you?

Z-Victor Two. Over.

What's bugging you, Christine! Those guys belong in the slammer. So why the long face? Level with ~e, will you? Christine – I thought we were friends!

Television Drama Serials

Titles

Angels
General Hospital
The Doctors
Emergency-Ward 10
Coronation Street
Flamingo Road
Peyton Place
Brookside
Crossroads
Emmerdale Farm
Take the High Road

Storylines

Births, marriages, deaths.

Hospital drama.

Torrid affairs.

Favourite characters, unjustly accused of serious crimes and only exonerated after much difficulty and personal suffering.

Sudden disasters – a fire, a burst gas main, an outbreak of foot-rot, the detonation of a wartime bomb that has lain dormant beneath the foundations for decades, redundancy, bankruptcy, invasion by squatters, Scottish soccer supporters or Hell's Angels.

Car accidents.

Poison pen letters.

Social comment – alcoholism, abortion, the plight of the homeless, the problems of the handicapped, adult literacy, unemployment, juvenile delinquency, life in the high-rise flats, education, child care and recreation.

Animal or pet sagas.

Comic interludes about learning to drive, going on holiday, marital disharmony, unexpected visitors, mistaken identity, the purchase of problematic cars or other items, wins at bingo or on the pools, trying to sell something unsaleable, putting on a Christmas panto, or coming unstuck in the act of painting a house, doing someone a good turn or trying to raise money for charity.

Characters

Mother-figures and father-figures.

Problem kids of all ages.

Old folk pouring scorn on today's standards.

Loose women with wandering eyes.

Operators, fixers, con men, masters of chat, rough diamonds.

The new doctor, nurse, consultant, patient who immediately signals the arrival of a new romance.

Figures from the past or unwanted relatives who descend unannounced and throw a whole community into turmoil.

Comic waitresses, barmaids, receptionists, shop assistants, nurses, secretaries and other menials with a line in saucer-eyed surprise and outraged innocence.

224

Comic barmen, porters, dossers, policemen, farmworkers, poachers, caretakers and other 'common men' who can pad out the areas between dramatic action with harmless humour.

The independent New Woman who makes it on her own in a masculine world by running a motel, a pub, a veterinary practice, a business, a department, a farm or a nightclub.

The star-crossed lovers who endure great miseries before finally triumphing over the cruel circumstances that fate has decreed should separate them.

The mystery newcomer ('We don't know much about him really. Keeps himself to himself') who acts as a catalyst in a small community, and who invariably turns out to be the exact opposite of what everyone had expected.

Dialogue
Nurse Rover's Return to the Emmerdale Motel at Brookside.

Episode 100,000.

Scene 13. Int. bar early evening.

(For the sake of convenience the entire cast is present. Establishing wide-shot to show cliché postures. The door opens and in walks Nurse Rover. General surprise.)

All: Eh, heck!/Well, would you ever!/Happen it *is* our kid, after all/This *is* a surprise!/What brings you back to the hospital?/Kill the fatted calf – she's back home!/You don't look a day older, love/I'd never have believed it!/Blimey!/And to think the last time I saw her, she was only knee-high to a grass hopper!/This is the best present a mother could have/Come to your Uncle Albert, dear!/Is it . . . no, it can't be!

Nurse: I just happened to be passing and thought I'd drop in!

Hilda: Eh, you look a bit peeky, chuck. Doesn't she, Stanley?

Ena: Summat's up wi' her. Don't stand there gawping, Annie Walker. Give the lass a drink.

Amos: Hold your horses, Mrs Sharples. I'll thank you to remember that *I* rule the roost behind the bar of the Woolpack. Let's observe some of the civilities, if you don't mind!

David: The Crossroads Motel can rise to the occasion, if duty calls. I'm asserting my voting rights on the Board – double brandies all round. (*Ad libbed thanks from all and sundry*)

Nurse: Thank you, Mr Hunter. You're a gentleman. (*She sits*). I'm sure you can guess the real reason I took the high road and came back to Brookside.

Henry: Aye. Because they had another crop failure on the Triangle Shipping Line while sailing via Flamingo Road.

Diane: Oo, no, Mr Wilks. Flipping heck! It's because she heard that Heather Huntington wanted someone to take her to the Accountant's Christmas Ball at Demdyke Row.

Donald: I believe the Church can throw some light on this. She has returned to the fold because her *ménage a trois* with Doris Luke and Mike Baldwin fell on stony ground.

Nurse: It's worse than that, vicar.

Adam: Benny hasn't made you pregnant again, has he?

Nurse: No, Mr Chance. After I gave birth to Ken Barlow's last set of twins, the scriptwriters had me sterilised. I'd be as right as rain if I wasn't so down in the dumps. I simply must tell *somebody*, Eudora, or I'll go stark, staring mad.

Bet: Spit it out, love. We're used to bad news around here. We've had two arrests, three divorces and a suicide already this week. And it were in that very seat that Len Fairclough told us that he were really Annie Sugden in drag. Use my shoulder to cry on. A friend in need is a friend indeed.

Nurse: They can't do this to me, Bet. If they think I'll knuckle under, they've got another think coming. I've sweated blood for them. I've been the scarlet woman and the toast of the town and the conscience of the Street and the secret drinker and the unmarried mother and the heroin addict and the comic relief and the heartbroken widow and the incurable gambler and the beautiful, blind girl and the cantankerous old ward sister and the dizzy blonde and Salvation Army girl. (*Weeps*). But in the next episode . . . I have a slight cold.

Matt: By God! They're writing her out! It's the end of soap opera as we know it!

Theme Music and Credits.

Light entertainment

Light entertainment is a playroom in which unruly artistes are locked and told to amuse themselves with toys, games and musical instruments. Anything goes, it's strictly for fun, and the sky's the limit. No harm can come to the fixtures and fittings. The formats are indestructible, the routines have stood the test of time, and the jokes will not break no matter how many times they are cracked. Life is a barrel of laughs.

Variety invariably sticks to the tried and trusted – begin with the dancers, end with the star, let the compère introduce the

227

acts in between. When the show is built around an individual, that performer must dominate from start to finish, introduce his or her own guests, and keep them in subjection either by singing with them or sending them up in a sketch. It is an unwritten law that the star must somehow be made to look more talented than anyone else. In *The Cilla Black Show*, for instance, Barbra Streisand would do a sword-swallowing act; if Bob Hope were to appear on *The Des O'Connor Hour*, he would be booked as a concert pianist.

Panel games are even more predictable. A quiz-master, four members of a panel, a simple question-and-answer routine and you're away. Because the quiz show involving innocent bystanders from the general public is a trifle more difficult, the presenter is always a patter merchant who can talk his way through any upsets. Clichés and catchphrases grow as high as an elephant's eye in this neck of the woods. The oldest trick in the book, of course, is to appeal to self-interest and dangle money, expensive gifts or the opportunity of showbiz stardom in front of the punters. Unseen by them, you will also be offering the chance to make a fool of themselves. It's a choice between Open The Box or Get Inside And We'll Bury You. Remember that it was the slaves who built the Pyramid Game.

Annual events like the Miss World Competition ('My ambition is to be the first woman President of America or to open a boutique') and the Eurovision Song Contest ('Can you hear me, Denmark? Will you give us your marks, please?') have their own particular clichés. It is a measure of their impact that in one fell swoop per year they have been able to impose those clichés on the smaller fry in the world of light entertainment. I shall announce the stereotypes in reverse order. In third place . . .

Titles

Game for a Laugh
Play Your Cards Right
Call My Bluff
That's Life
Tell the Truth
Give Us a Clue
What's My Line?

Cannon and Ball
Little and Large
3-2-1
This is Your Life
That Was the Week That Was
The Good Old Days
Top of the Pops

Formats

Variety.

Pop stars mime to their latest hits.

Quiz shows for telly celebrities.

Quiz shows for members of the Idiot Public.

Solo performer – Cliff, Shirley, Sinatra and so on – in concert with a perfect audience.

Chat shows hosted by 'personalities' who have failed to make it in any other branch of show business.

Comedy shows that rely on the willingness of ordinary people to be mocked and humiliated in public.

Circus.

Satire.

Entertainment posing as an investigative organisation with the public interest at heart.

Telling someone's life story and missing out all the interesting bits.

Opportunity Knocks and other misnomers.

Characters

Genuine stars.

Variety artistes with set routines.

Famous faces that fit on panel games.

People who will do anything to get on telly and have the chance to win paltry prizes by answering questions ('Who wrote Handel's Largo?') that do not tax the brain.

Oily and urbane quiz-masters and presenters who know by instinct at which camera they must mug at any given moment.

Hapless victims who are persuaded that they are 'good sports' because they allow some cruel practical joke that has been played on them to be screened for the watching millions.

Fading stars who make a fading comeback as part of the wallpaper in the story of someone else's life.

Circus artistes.

University graduates who confuse the act of making fun of others with true satire.

Callous and self-promoting showbiz celebrities who sit in judgement on new performers, and do their best to discourage them from joining the profession.

The studio audience.

Guests on chat shows who come along in the mistaken belief that they are the audience-grabbers rather than their hosts.

Orchestra conductors who get in on the act.

Dialogue

How tickled I am today!

Bernie, the bolt.

You'll like this. Not a lot . .

It's not the jokes, it's the way I tell them.

What do you think of the show so far?
  – Rubbish!

John Smith, explorer, archaeologist, gun-runner, sex maniac, Britain's most wanted man – This Is Your Life!

Rock on, Tommy!

Didn't he do well!

By Jove, I needed that!

Hello, good evening and welcome . . .

I wanna tell you a story.

What a gay day! They all owe me money . . . Shut that door!

There's no answer to that.

Oriel College, your starter for ten. No conferring . . .

And now for something completely different.

A funny thing happened to me on my way to the studio . . .

Viewers at home will be able to see the answers on their screens now.

Up a bit, down a bit, left a bit, right a bit . . .

Ladies and gentlemen, introducing, for your delight and delectation, a triumph of the Terpsichorean, an essay in equilibrium and equipoise . . .

So please give a warm welcome to some more friends who are willing to play the Generation Game!

And now, we'd like to sing you our latest single which is riding high in the charts and is called . . .

My next guest has been described as a poor man's Michael Parkinson and a rich man's Russell Harty. He's been at the top for the whole of his career and is now celebrating two hundred consecutive years in showbiz. Ladies and gentlemen, who else could it be but . . .

Sport

Sport embraces all aspects of television. It is News ('And we've just heard that the World 1500 metres record has been broken in Oslo for the eighth time this week'). It deals with Current Affairs ('They have now sacked their manager because of his relationship with the wife of the club's physiotherapist'). It brings in Religion ('Just listen to those Welsh voices raised in song as their team heads for yet another Triple Crown'). It relies heavily on Situation Comedy ('He's lost his hat and his saddle now and is hanging on like grim death as Sanyo Anglezark Double Glazing Zanussi Crown Wallpapers Allied Carpet Sale II approaches this five-barred gate'). Education is ever-present ('Well, I've never seen *that* on a snooker table before! You live and learn!'). And Drama dominates ('And the streaker has eluded the policemen yet again!').

Sports is a Feature Documentary about national hysteria. It is an eternal Children's Programme posing as adult viewing. It is Light Entertainment of the lightest and most entertaining kind. It even trespasses on the property of the Video Nastie ('And his head has now disappeared completely between the thighs of Giant Haystacks!'). Sport is the cup that cheers, the Empire of the Early Bath, the Diocese of the Dropped Catch. It is a Jump-Orff Against the Clock. All human life is there but it is reduced to a series of action replays.

Commentators have been unfairly criticised for talking in clichés, for getting over-excited, and for making too many mistakes in the heat of the moment. Nobody reflects his material more honestly than the sports commentator. Clichés are in the nature of the beast. Sport is bound hand and foot by rules and regulations. It is temperamentally over-excited. It thrives on mistakes and hasty misjudgements. To try to impose new standards and new clichés on the commentator is simply a case of carrying Colemans to Newcastle. Fallibility is all. Sportsmanship is human error.

The stage is set for a pulsating section here with perfect

weather conditions, packed terraces and four men in the wall. And the referee blows his whistle and gets us away . . .

Sporting Types

Footballer – Tommy laid it off to me, I played a one-two with Danny then slipped it wide to Billy, he took it to the by-line and crossed it, Terry got his head to it, the keeper palmed it down, there was a goalmouth scramble and I got the touch that mattered.

Football Manager – This game is all about scoring goals. They took their chances and we didn't, but we were still the best team on the park. Ian Wallace was very unlucky to be sent off for stabbing their sweeper and Gary Birtles should have got a penalty when he was brought down in the box.

Rugby Union Captain – Concentration and discipline. Play the game in their half. Pressurise them. Go through on their rubbish ball and kick seven barrels of shit out of anyone who falls on it.

Champion Boxer – Yeah, Harry, I did, Harry. Knew I'd win when I had him in trouble in the third, Harry. He was a good fighter and could punch a bit, Harry, but I was getting in a lot of shots, working to the body, Harry, know what I mean? Yeah, I showed him who was gaffer in that ring tonight . . .

Boxing Manager – Joe Bugner is the finest heavyweight prospect that this country has ever produced.

Showjumper – She's a big, scopey horse and she decided that this was going to be her night.

Athlete – It went exactly to plan. I let him tow me around for the first three laps, sat on his shoulder down the back strait, then kicked for home with two hundred metres to go. He had nothing left.

Snooker Player – It's always nice to have a Championship under your belt this early in the season. Steve is the man to beat and I beat him.

Tennis Star – *Out?* Aw, come one! Come on! That was on the line! Don't you know chalk dust when you see it!

Winning Jockey – Ah, he's a grand hoss. I gave him a tickle two furlongs from home and it was all over bar the shouting. The heavy going really suited him . . .

Test Cricketer – Difficult to explain, really. I swung the bat and it kept hitting the ball. Just one of those days. Cricket's a bit like that sometimes.

Motor Racing Ace – You learn to live with the danger.

Cliché Commentary

Welcome to Anfield, where the atmosphere is electric as we await this Battle of the Giants between Liverpool, six points clear at the top of the Cannon League, and Manchester United, hot on their heels, and unbeaten in their last six games. Your referee today is Martin Davey from Bury St Edmund's and if Alex Higgins can pot this red and come off the baulk cushion to kiss the yellow, we could be in for a real surprise. Desmond Douglas is going to have to pull out all the stops and play his best table tennis if he is to stop Big Daddy winning by a fall and a submission in the last round at Wentworth.

And that's the kind of tactics you'd expect from a Welsh team. Typically ebullient rugby which keeps them in the hunt as they cut the deficit to three points. And the big question is can Dusty Hare jump this wall again? The time to beat is forty-five seconds and there's Harvey Smith watching his arch-rival and signalling that there are two more balls in this over. Geoff Lawson to bowl to Ian Botham and see if he can stop the rot. And as Lawson comes running in from the Nursery End, it might be time to bring in Dan Maskell for his comments on that amazing double-fault.

It's Wayward Lad still leading from Sailor Joe with Melchior pressing hard on the outside and Bluebell's Folly making a run on the inside. Then comes Duke of Dundee, Coriander and Passionella with Steve Ovett the backmarker. And that was as perfect an exhibition of ice-skating as you're ever likely to see and – yes – maximum points from all the judges, with the exception of the Russian. But can Woodcock finish? Yes! It's there! Tony Woodcock has put the ball in the net and British cyclists have won their first gold medal in these championships. A single basket separates the two teams as we come to the final quarter and it's all down to Nick Faldo to get maximum points on the parallel bars.

There'll be cheers down in Neath if he kicks this one and helps to stem the Irish tide but no – still off target – Fatima Whitbread has obviously left her kicking boots at home. This is vintage hockey, end-to-end stuff and full of goalmouth incident. But the ball goes high, wide and handsome and lands in that bunker to the left of the green. Such is the beauty of golf! But Magri is not finished yet. A left hook to the head and a good right under the heart – just listen to those cheers from the packed crowd here at the Winter Olympics. Because this is the acid test for our swimmers. Can they hold off the challenge of the Denver Broncos as time starts to run out?

Cathy's got a useful Jamaican inside her as she comes round this bend and she's left herself a lot of running to do, but West Ham are using a bit of width now and closing down the Everton midfield. Chris Tavaré pads that away and he's beginning to get a slow hand clap from the crowd. And Billie Jean King, the uncrowned queen of Wimbledon, knows that she has to clear all the colours to win because the McLaren is breathing down her neck and Tom Watson has still got three more holes to play. Forest throw. A little chip. Huyton's header. Todd read that well. Good one-touch stuff, this. But the Australian yacht is closing fast on Steve Cram. There's the bell and it's anybody's race now as Andy Irvine manufactures a kick to touch and the British pair have a bit of room to work in.

The cross is coming in once more, the defenders have taken up deep positions, Terry Griffiths is pulling into the pits, Bob Willis has cleared the water jump, Lester Piggott is taking a compulsory count of nine, Jack Nicklaus scores another basket and – yes! they've done it! Oxford have won the 400th Boat Race in record time! This is what rowing is all about!

Afterword

Churchill once said of a speech by Sir Anthony Eden that it contained every known cliché except God Is Love and Please Adjust Your Dress Before Leaving. *The Finest Swordsman In All France* does not claim to be quite so comprehensive. Though it has tried to pick the sweetest forbidden fruit in the Garden of Eden, it is all too conscious of leaving such choice apples as these unpicked:

'I've had my fill of empty pockets, Captain.'

The Molly Maguires.

'The whole of Cambridge holds its breath. If this kick goes over, it will put the game back in the melting-pot.'

Rugby Special. **Nigel Starmer-Smith.**

Whatever else he was – and his virtues were many – Mr Wang of Shanghai was a superb liar. He was not a Chinaman for nothing.

Secret Society of the Tortoise Mask. **Major Charles Gilson.**

New Leader's bid to steer Labour off rocks. Captain Kinnock sets sail for No. 10.

Sunday People. October 2, 1983.

'Boil some water – lots of it.'
It was a good line. It had sprung to his mind full grown as soon as he had read the script.

The Pat Hobby Stories. **F Scott Fitzgerald.**

'There was sights a man must thank his Maker he'll never see in this land.'

By The Sword Divided.

'Nay, man,' said the Prince, 'my lips are sealed! And the members of the league jealously guard the secret of their chief ... so his fair adorers have to be content with worshipping a shadow. Here in England, Monsieur,' he added, with wonderful charm and dignity, 'we but name the Scarlet Pimpernel, and every fair cheek is suffused with a blush of enthusiasm. None have seen him save his faithful lieutenants. We know not if he be tall or short, fair or dark, handsome or ill-formed; but we know that he is the bravest gentleman in all the world, and we all feel a little proud, Monsieur, when we remember that he is an Englishman.'

The Scarlet Pimpernel. **Baroness Orczy.**

The origin of this book is lost in the mists of time, place and action. But it ends as it began: with the belief that clichés are made in heaven.

Epilogue

**THE GLITTERING PHRASES OF TODAY
ARE THE
CLICHÉS OF TOMORROW**

The
HYPOCHONDRIAC'S
HANDBOOK

DR. LEE SCHREINER
DR. GEORGE THOMAS

The Health Service prides itself on its ability to care for the sick – but what provision is there for the misunderstood minority, the hypochondriacs? Unfairly discriminated against by the entire medical profession, they are continually denied the attention they so obviously *deserve* . . .

At long last, THE HYPOCHONDRIAC'S HANDBOOK redresses the balance. An invaluable aid to all sufferers from imaginary illnesses, it tells of a host of alarming and hideous ailments which may befall the permanent malingerer at any time, plus how to fake symptoms when the disease is not actually contracted. You'll never feel safe again, once you've discovered which Life Threatening Infections You Can Catch From Your Pets . . . how Physical Fitness is Hazardous to Your Health . . . How to Recognise Your Own Psychiatric Emergencies . . . and The Hypochondriac's Guide to Sexual Dysfunctions!

HUMOUR   0 7221 7720 8   £1.50

The Book Of
ROYAL
LISTS

CRAIG BROWN & LESLEY CUNLIFFE

What should you serve the Royal Family if they drop in for dinner?
How does the Queen keep her Corgies content?
Which clergyman did Prince Charles throw into the fountain at Balmoral?
What are Princess Diana's favourite sweets?
Which television programmes does the Queen Mother like best?
How can you recognise a Royal racing pigeon?

The Royal Family is no ordinary family, and Royal Lists are not like ordinary lists. Here at last are the answers to all the questions that have intrigued dedicated Royal-watchers, loyal patriots, convinced monarchists and the millions of adoring fans around the world who follow every move of Britain's first family.

THE BOOK OF ROYAL LISTS is the most comprehensive collection of information ever assembled about the British Royal Family and their ancestors. Witty and informed, amusing but respectful, it surprises, charms and dazzles.

HUMOUR   0 7221 1934 8   £2.50

A SELECTION OF BESTSELLERS FROM SPHERE

FICTION

CHANGES	Danielle Steel	£1.95 ☐
FEVRE DREAM	George R. R. Martin	£2.25 ☐
LADY OF FORTUNE	Graham Masterton	£2.75 ☐
FIREFOX DOWN	Craig Thomas	£2.25 ☐
MAN OF WAR	John Masters	£2.50 ☐

FILM & TV TIE-INS

THE DUNE STORYBOOK	Joan Vinge	£2.50 ☐
INDIANA JONES AND THE TEMPLE OF DOOM	James Kahn	£1.75 ☐
ONCE UPON A TIME IN AMERICA	Lee Hays	£1.75 ☐
SUPERGIRL	Norma Fox Mazer	£1.75 ☐
MINDER – BACK AGAIN	Anthony Masters	£1.50 ☐

NON-FICTION

THE YOUNG ONES' BOOK	Rik Mayall, Ben Elton & Lise Mayer	£2.95 ☐
WORST MOVIE POSTERS OF ALL TIME	Greg Edwards	£4.95 ☐
THE AGE OF DINOSAURS – A PHOTOGRAPHIC RECORD	Jane Burton & Dougal Dixon	£5.95 ☐
THE FINEST SWORDSMAN IN ALL FRANCE	Keith Miles	£1.95 ☐
POLITICAL QUOTES	Michael Rogers	£1.50 ☐

All Sphere books are available at your local bookshop or newsagent, or can be ordered direct from the publisher. Just tick the titles you want and fill in the form below.

Name_____

Address_____

_____

Write to Sphere Books, Cash Sales Department, P.O. Box 11, Falmouth, Cornwall TR10 9EN
Please enclose a cheque or postal order to the value of the cover price plus:
UK: 45p for the first book, 20p for the second book and 14p per copy for each additional book ordered to a maximum charge of £1.63.
OVERSEAS: 75p for the first book plus 21p per copy for each additional book.
BFPO & EIRE: 45p for the first book, 20p for the second book plus 14p per copy for the next 7 books, thereafter 8p per book.

Sphere Books reserve the right to show new retail prices on covers which may differ from those previously advertised in the text or elsewhere, and to increase postal rates in accordance with the PO.